THE MONEY CHAMP'S GUIDE TO

GETTING A COLLEGE DEGREE
Debt Free

Disclaimer

The links or websites in this book are provided for informational purposes only and do not constitute an endorsement of any products or services provided by these websites and that the links are subject to change, expire, or be redirected without any notice.

THE MONEY CHAMP'S GUIDE TO

GETTING A COLLEGE DEGREE
Debt Free

NICK BLAIR

Copyright © 2016 Nick Blair
All rights reserved.

All rights reserved. No part of this publication may be reproduced, distributed, or transmitted in any form or by any means, including photocopying, recording, or other electronic or mechanical methods, without the prior written permission of the publisher, except in the case of brief quotations embodied in critical reviews and certain other non-commercial uses permitted by copyright law. For permission requests, write to the publisher, at the address below.

Nick@theMoneyChamp.com
www.theMoneyChamp.com

Book Cover Design by GSPH
Book Layout & Design by JP Kusmin

First Printed, October 2016
ISBN-13: 978-1539676997

Acknowledgment

Every accomplishment in life has the cooperation and effort of many gifted and talented individuals that come together for a common purpose. This book is no different. GOD amazes me how he places the right people in your life at the right time! I am eternally grateful for all my hardships and experiences, whether good or bad because this book is a culmination of those experiences.

First, I want to thank GOD for placing my purpose inside of me and for birthing this publication out of me. Without him, all of my success is not possible.

Second, I want to thank my parents Stanley and Harriel Blair. My Father who is a veteran of the United States Air Force and retiree from Tennessee Valley Authority and my Mother who is a retired Educator instilled the values, morals, integrity, dedication and were great examples of how to live for GOD and do things the right way. I will never be able to express the level of gratitude that you two are so deserving of.

Third, I want to thank my beautiful and beloved wife Amanda for always being in my corner and supporting me in whatever I take on. Thank you for understanding my vision and assignment and granting me the time to take on this project. You are truly a virtuous woman and I am so lucky to have you.

Next, let me give thanks to my beautiful, creative and wonderful daughter A'Yannah. You are also heaven sent and definitely keep me young by keeping me on my toes.

Finally, a big thank you goes out to my business partner Jonathan Taylor who kept things in order and helped guide this project from start to finish. Jonathan truly took me and my book under his wing and really made this possible. Also a huge thanks to Kirsten Oschwald for the incredible job she did of proofing, editing and re-writing sections of this manuscript.

And a special thanks to my family, friends, coworkers, & colleagues.

Contents

Chapter 1
INTRODUCTION 1
- AN EPIDEMIC 4
- Student Loan Debt Crisis 6
- Effects of Student Debt... 9
- Education is the Key 10
- Loan "Prevention Principles" for Students 11

Chapter 2
YOUR STRENGTHS AND PURPOSE:
FIRST THINGS FIRST 13
- Self-Discovery through Coaching 16
- Career/Job Fairs and Job Shadowing 18
- Gap Year 19
- UnCollege 20
- Purpose Leads to Productivity 22
- Selecting a School 25
- Choosing a Major 27
- EDUsquared 29
- Future Earnings 32

Chapter 3
SCHOLARSHIPS, GRANTS, AND
OTHER SOURCES OF MONEY 37
- Student Financial Outlook 37

- Family Contributions 38
- "GIFT" AID 40
- Scholarships 40
- Grants 41
- Federal Pell Grant 41
- Benefits for Military Service 43
- College Prep Ready 44
- State Scholarships 47
- College Track 47
- Universal Principles 48
- College Prep Genius 49
- Additional Scholarship Strategies 55

Chapter 4
NON-TRADITIONAL CREDIT:
SAVE THOUSANDS 59

- Advanced Placement and
  International Baccalaureate Courses 60
- College Level Examination Program 61
- ACE Alternative Credit 61
- Online Courses and Programs 62
- Dual Enrollment 63

Chapter 5
GENERATE ADDITIONAL INCOME
WHILE IN COLLEGE 65

- Federal Work-Study 66
- Full-Time Benefits 69
- Talent Pool 71

Chapter 6
MONEY MANAGEMENT AND SAVINGS STRATEGIES . 73

- Savings Strategy 74

- Making the Best of It 77
- Cost-Cutting Strategies 78

Chapter 7
SOMETIMES DEBT HAPPENS:
PATHWAYS TO DEBT FREEDOM 85

- Student Loan Management Principles 85
- Repaying Your Loans 87
- Traditional Repayment Plans 91
- Income-Driven Repayment Plans 93
- Loan Consolidation 96
- Deferment and Forbearance 96
- Loan Forgiveness, Cancellation, and Discharge 97
- Total and Permanent Disability (TPD) Discharge 98
- Death Discharge 98
- Discharge in Bankruptcy 99
- Teacher Loan Forgiveness 99
- Public Service Loan Forgiveness 100
- Perkins Loan Cancellation and Discharge 100
- Late or Missed Payments 101
- Default 101
- Resolve Loan Problems Quickly 102
- Jaideep's Story (part 2): 103
- Refinancing….or Not 104
- Debt Free After Three.. 105

Chapter 8
FINAL THOUGHTS 109

❖

CHAPTER 1

INTRODUCTION

This book has been in the making for 33 years. Yes, you read that correctly—33 years. It took longer than expected to come to fruition, because like many people, I didn't know what I was supposed to be doing with my life until I turned 33. This project took longer, cost more, and involved far more decisions, risks, faith, and prayer than I could have ever imagined. And I have loved every minute of it.

I feel the need to share my story to help others navigate through the higher education process - to avoid the traps and pitfalls that have claimed so many victims. As of 2016, 43 million Americans have fallen into the student-loan debt predicament.

I know.... I was one of them. I didn't take middle school, and especially high school, very seriously. I was focused on what many young boys are focused on—girls and sports. I didn't understand the importance of figuring out what I wanted to be when I grew up, so I could take the right classes that interested me - ones that would help me get to where I was going, and get there the most efficiently.

I did not have the focus, desire, or direction I needed to want to be the best version of me, because I had no clue what I wanted to do with my life. In hindsight, I believe that had I known my purpose then, I would have taken a businesslike approach when it came to school and my grades. I have never been afraid of hard work, but I must see the return on investment to be motivated.

In school, I was a smart person, but I couldn't find anyone to help me unlock my true identity and unleash my passion on the world! I needed someone to "connect the dots" for the things I was passionate about—what I needed to learn and how to get there. If I had had that, I firmly believe I would not have needed to take out student loans, because I would have done the hard work and received scholarships. As it was, I took out loan after loan, never trying to secure scholarships or grants, simply out of sheer laziness. I was more interested in hanging out with friends, having fun, and working. Even though I worked a full-time job while in school, I decided to buy a new car and other things I didn't need because, at the time, having that was more important than repaying my debt and starting my professional career on the best foot possible.

So I ended up graduating from the University of Tennessee at Chattanooga with a degree in Sports Management, with about $25,000 of student-loan debt. Compared to some, who have well over $100,000 of student loan debt, my $25,000 doesn't seem like a lot, but it had a profound impact on my life. As a result, I have become a debt-fighter, and I created the *Money Champ* to help people "win in the financial ring with money."

CHAPTER 1: INTRODUCTION

As the saying goes, now I am "older and wiser." Older, definitely. Wiser...hopefully!

Some things to consider:

As a parent, do you feel incapable of or unsure about helping your child prepare for college? How will you pay for college? As a student, do you really have the desire and drive to attend and graduate from college?

This book has something for everyone—whether you're a middle school or high school student, parent, college student, or college grad! In *The Money Champ's Guide to Getting a College Degree Debt Free*, I give you the blueprint on how to attend college without falling into substantial debt as well as ways to earn an income while you are there.

Through sharing my personal story and knowledge, podcast interviews, dozens of tips, strategies, and resources, I desire to show you the key to success. In this book, you will discover:

- The proper way to prepare financially for college
- How to find your area of interest before you graduate high school
- Strategies on picking the right classes for your future
- How to find and get the best and most advantageous scholarships and grants
- Creative ways to generate more income while in college
- Money and time-management principles and savings strategies
- Real-life scenarios to think through and role play

You will learn why the "conventional wisdom," which is so deeply ingrained in our society, is wrong when it comes to getting a college degree. This conventional wisdom asserts that:

- Student loans are a good form of debt. They are a necessary investment, and they won't have a negative impact on borrower's lives.
- It is unreasonable to expect students to be able to pay for college on their own.
- The name of the college or university on a graduate's diploma will have a big impact on their career success.
- Only top athletes and students with the best grades actually win scholarships.
- The competition for scholarships is too stiff for "regular" students to apply.

My hope is that by the time you finish reading, you will understand that each of these statements just isn't true. I am grateful you have picked up this book, and I hope that the hard-earned wisdom I share in the following pages will motivate and help you to achieve the goal of "Getting a College Degree—Debt Free"! I welcome your questions or comments at Nick@theMoneyChamp.com.

AN EPIDEMIC

A financial epidemic has been sweeping through America for decades, and it has reached a fever pitch—student loan debt. A student loan is a form of financial aid that is designed to help students pay for university tuition, books, and living expenses. However, in some ways, student loans can be considered predatory loans, similar to those found in subprime mortgage lending. There are few restrictions on who can borrow (in this case, for higher education), and little consideration is given to whether or not a borrower can repay. Job and credit status do not matter—the loan is not secured by anything tangible. In other words, a student loan is an unsecured loan, given with no credit check, that's available to anyone 18 or older who may or may not have the resources or a plan to repay the debt.

I hate the student loans process. I want to rid the world of the current student loans process. I have had them myself, and I know what it is like to have to pay them back. In essence, they are the only type of loan available that is unsecured, not even requiring a credit check or collateral or even that the borrower has a job or source of income. Of course, there is some responsibility on the student's part but, for all intents and purposes, all that a student has to do is be eighteen years old and have a pulse, and he or she can borrow enough money to negatively impact their future financial stability for years.

The cost of higher education keeps going up every year. According to data from the U.S. Department of Labor, college tuition is the fastest growing household expense, and the cost of attending a public or private college will continue to soar. From January 2006 to July 2016, the Consumer Price Index for college tuition and fees increased 63 percent, compared with an increase of 21 percent for all household budget items in general. Over that period, consumer prices for college textbooks increased 88 percent and housing at school (excluding board) increased 51 percent.[1]

According to the College Board, the average cost of tuition and fees for the 2015–2016 school year was $32,405 at private colleges, $9,410 for state residents at public colleges, and $23,893 for out-of-state residents attending public universities. This does *not* include housing and meals, which is a substantial expense on its own.[2] By 2030, at current rates of increase, the price tag for tuition at a private college will inflate to $102,086, with $45,589 being the cost for public universities. A newborn child today can expect to pay $440,000 in total for a private college education by the time he or she attends, if the current trends continue.

So, from the time we start school, we are told that to be successful in life we have to get a college degree...but the college degree is generally not affordable. This certainly seems like a great way to ensure that this financial sector keeps bringing in the money. As noted in Chapter 7 of this book, it is very hard to get out from under student loan debt by filing for bankruptcy. The government and student loan lending companies make sure that they get their money, one way or the other. Unsecured student loans are probably the least risky loans to the lender, compared to other unsecured loans, since government and private student loan lending companies have their loans guaranteed against default. This means that in many cases, American taxpayers are ultimately the ones bearing the cost when overextended students default.

Economists have warned for years that a higher education bubble is forming, and that if it bursts, it could perpetrate widespread damage on the economy, similar to the subprime mortgage lending bubble which led to the 2008 financial crisis and "Great Recession." Data from the Department of Education shows that the student loan default rate has been rising steadily since 2005.

Student Loan Debt Crisis

In just the first three months of 2013, government and private student loan defaults were the most in United States history. According to the U.S. Department of Education, 6.8 million federal student loan borrowers are now in default, representing $85 billion in debt.[3] This higher education debt crisis is hanging over the heads of both recent and longstanding graduates, as well as students who never finished their education. Currently, the average student loan debt is close to $30,000. About 70 percent of 2013 graduates left college with an average of $28,400 in debt.

According to the Federal Reserve Bank of New York, here are some other unsettling facts:[4]

- Student debt is large, and appears to have significant effects on macroeconomic outcomes (household formation, homeownership, consumption)
- During and after the Great Recession, households reduced their other debts, but student loan balances continued to increase
- Because the majority of student loans are federal, tight bank lending standards did not affect student loans
- Between 2004 and 2014, there was an 89 percent increase in the number of borrowers and a 77 percent increase in the average balance size
- Borrowers who left school during the Great Recession had particular difficulty with their student loan repayment, with many defaulting, becoming seriously delinquent, or not being able to reduce their balance
- Borrowers from lower and middle-income areas, as well as borrowers who originated loans in their thirties, are at greater risk of default and delinquency
- The low overall repayment rate helps explain the steady growth in aggregate student debt, now at nearly 1.2 trillion dollars

Total student loan balances by age group

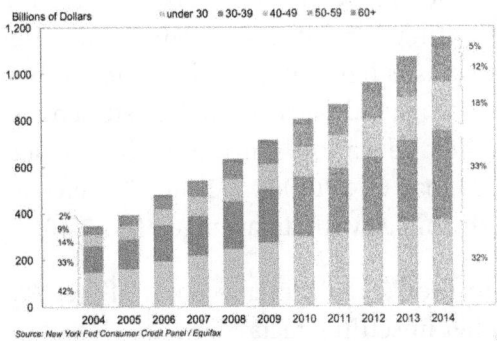

Student loans defy business cycle

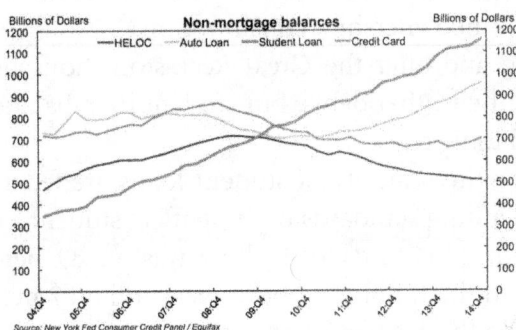

Defaults and default rate

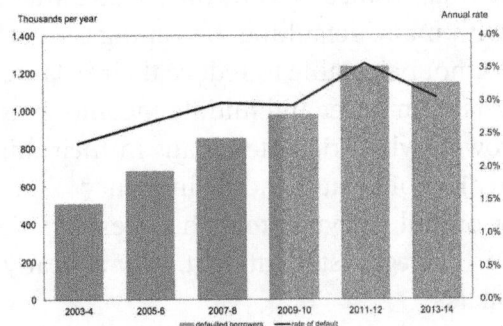

Effects of Student Debt

The American Student Assistance organization carried out a study in 2013, which confirmed some disheartening facts about the effects of education debt.

> Student loan debt is having a profound impact on the daily lives and spending habits of young Americans, casting a pall over the nation's economic recovery. Many borrowers may never run into problems with their loans, but the mere existence of the debt is a burden that is impacting the way student borrowers make important lifestyle decisions. Those with student debt are delaying decisions to buy a home, get married, have children, save for retirement, and enter a desired career field because of their debt. This downward spiral has a cascading impact on the nation's economy as the generation charged with investing in the nation's future is delaying their lives because of student debt. Student loans were created to be an engine for social mobility, but they are, in fact, limiting young people's ability to achieve financial success.[5]

A recent 2016 study conducted by the National Foundation for Credit Counseling[6] found that, of those people currently paying on outstanding educational loan debt, a total of 53 percent feel that their debt prevents them from either saving for retirement, purchasing a car, or putting money away for an emergency fund. A total of 35 percent struggle to pay either the monthly debt payment or for basic necessities like rent or food and utilities. The influence that educational debt has on individuals, their families, and their communities cannot be overstated—it goes far beyond whether specific borrowers are just able to make their student loan payments. There are repercussions both for immediate personal finance decisions and for lifetime financial well-being.

Education is the Key

Pursuing higher education in today's world requires much thought, consideration, education, and planning in the financing process, by parents, students, guidance counselors, financial advisors, and whoever else you trust that is willing to help. As a society, we research and educate ourselves before we take out a mortgage or car loan and before we invest in stocks and other financial vehicles. We even research smartphones before we make a purchase and we are only going to have that device for two or three years.

Why would we not do the research to educate ourselves about student loans? If taken out irresponsibly, it will take a good portion, if not the rest of our lives, to pay them off? We *must* gain an in-depth understanding of the different types of loans, interest rates, grants, and scholarships available, principles to prevent needing loans in the first place, and all possible management and forgiveness options.

Then, after we educate ourselves on the student loan process, we must ask ourselves a few tough questions:
- Is a student loan *really* worth it?
- What other alternatives besides a loan do I have or does my child have?
- What can I do as a parent to ensure my child's dreams of pursuing higher education and getting a good start afterwards are realized?

- What kind of financial contribution is expected of me as a parent?

It is very disheartening to ascertain that, due to this loan epidemic, pursuing higher education is an undeniably risky investment.

The Money Champ's Guide to Getting a College Degree Debt Free can help future students, parents, and current borrowers to minimize the risk of taking out student loans, and in many cases, it will eliminate the need for student loans altogether by educating and empowering readers. This book will aid parents and potential students in 1) developing a financial strategy to fund college by educating you about student loans, and 2) helping you to discover your child's purpose and passion in life so that he or she can hit the ground running their first year with *direction* and a major or field of study already selected. Methods are described in this book which will help you prevent the need to take out loans. It also provides students with information and resources for grants, scholarships, and work-study options to minimize, if not eliminate, the risk of student loans.

Loan "Prevention Principles" for Students

- Discover your purpose and pursue your passion to ensure you are only considering universities or colleges that provide your future major.
- Once you identify the school(s) for you, utilize your high school counselor, higher education financial aid office(s), the Internet, and resources such as this book to search for grants, scholarships, and work-study opportunities to help pay tuition costs.

- With the help of parents, guardians, high school counselors, college coaches, or someone you trust, create a sound financial plan on how to pay for college. All situations are different and specific to each student.
- If you know you want to pursue higher education and will need substantial financial assistance for school, either get a part-time job as soon as you are able, or make finding and applying for scholarships your part-time job. Save as much of each paycheck as feasible. It is never too early to start gathering money for college.
- If possible, work at places that offer tuition assistance or company-provided scholarships for eligible workers (for example, Chick-fil-A, Apple Store, and Starbucks, or the college you will attend).

Throughout this book, you will encounter discussions, comments, and advice from a number of college graduates who have traveled the path and successfully navigated the pitfalls of college financing. My hope is that you will find value in their experiences and take the nuggets of wisdom within their stories to heart as you walk this road and take on these challenges yourself.

CHAPTER 2

YOUR STRENGTHS AND PURPOSE: FIRST THINGS FIRST

Every person on this Earth has a purpose for their existence. If you do not know your purpose in life, how will you know what to major in? How will you know what career field suits you best? How will you get through college without spending a fortune?

According to CollegeAtlas, 70 percent of Americans will study at a four-year college, but less than two-thirds will graduate. Regrettably, 30 percent of college and university students drop out after their first year.[1]

There are many reasons for this, but a major factor is that many of these students who left college were not in the correct field of study. A student who does not feel fulfilled or motivated is just going through the motions and will have a harder time putting in the effort to succeed.

For example, reading is not high on my list of favorite activities, but I really enjoy reading books, articles, and blogs about things I am passionate about or that interest me because there is a purpose for the reading. While I am reading that kind of material, without even realizing it, I quit focusing on the fact that I am reading. Another case in point—I absolutely hate to run just for the sake of running, but I love going outside and playing basketball, soccer, and football because there is a purpose behind the running. When I am playing sports, again, I completely forget about the fact that I also am doing something that isn't my favorite activity; I am just out there having fun.

I firmly believe that a lot of student loan debt stems from people not knowing their "why." Knowing your "why" is essentially knowing what makes you tick - your purpose and passion. As the old saying goes, "what do you want to be when you grow up?"

By knowing your "why," you discover your purpose. Once you know and understand your purpose, the passion for operating in your purpose will erupt and consume you! It is also very important to surround yourself with activities, things, and people that will plant the seeds of empowerment and guidance, which will help cultivate your skills and talents to assist you in pursuing your goals in life based on your purpose and passion. Discovering, cultivating, and operating within your purpose leads to fulfillment, which has enhanced the quality of life for millions of individuals. Discovering your "why" will motivate you and give you a "new lease on life" mentality!

As I was growing up, my dad worked for Tennessee Valley Authority, so he always used to dress up and wear a tie to work every day. I knew that I wanted to wear a tie to work and I wanted to dress up, and I knew that I did not want to work in a factory. There is absolutely nothing wrong with working in a factory, but I knew from an early age it wasn't for me. My inner core, dreams, and goals did not align with a factory position. It just was not in my DNA. I knew that I had a different calling on my life but, outside of that, I had no earthly idea what I wanted to do. My parents grew up in a time where education was preached and taught as the way to achieve your dreams and to have a good, pleasing, and comfortable lifestyle. Both of my parents have degrees, so not going to college was not really an option. I do remember them telling me that college was not for everybody and if I did not go to college, then I would have to find a trade. Manual labor has never been appealing to me, so from that conversation on, I knew I was going to college! They always supported me in whatever I wanted to do, but I just knew that in order to have a good lifestyle and to be well-off like my parents, I needed to go to college, but I didn't know what to do.

As a child, I loved sports, and I did whatever it took to be the best, no matter the cost, time, or effort required. There was no shortcut, easy way, or waving of a magic wand to be the best. I knew I had to make a sacrifice to put in the time and effort to be the best I could be—not always the best player, but that was my goal. In sports, I had the passion or love for it, with the purpose of being the best player out there. I had a vision, clear direction, motivation, and perseverance because I knew exactly what I wanted.

Unfortunately, I did not choose to put forth the same effort in searching and applying for college scholarships. I had no clear direction because I had no clue what I wanted to do with the rest of my life. Without recognizing the purpose for the rest of my life, I was not passionate about much in college (other than meeting girls), so I had no clear direction or vision for my life. No vision or clear direction resulted in no motivation or perseverance. I did not care, and it was much easier just to apply for a loan that would not be declined. All I had to do to receive a student loan was to wave the magic wand!

Self-Discovery through Coaching

Jennifer Bouley, of Bouley-Mak Consulting and Coaching, shares her philosophy that "life is not what happens to you, it is about how *you* can prepare and make change happen." She and her firm are committed to helping people (particularly pre-college and recent graduates) find their passions and their best career. Numerous times, she has seen situations where a person has a natural skill set in one area—cooking, for example—to the point that they could have a career as a chef. Instead, the parents or the family (or even the student) are pushing that person to do something else - like business or going into a trade because that's where the job prospects are. Ms. Bouley reminds us that we are never truly guaranteed success in any line of work and, at the end of the day, you are the one living in your skin, and you have to deal with it. It's not just about how much money you could make and whether or not you will get a job. No matter *what* you study, you can always find a job in it…it is in how you go about finding it.

Also, if you are not currently studying or working in your passion, it does not mean that you can't pursue your passion on the side. You can have a career you love or a job you like or that meets your needs in other ways, and you can also have things outside of work (that you could also make into a career) that you pursue as well.

She gives some valuable insight into the process her company uses to help clients find their passion:

> The first step is really getting down to the base values, the basic core: What are you interested in? What do you want out of your career? What do you see yourself doing in the next so-many years? We start to work to build a vision. Our clients go through two or three different career tests, which results in a grouping of suggested careers and institutions. The tests chiefly give them an overview of potential pitfalls in their career and the best environment for their individual needs and desires. Not every career is perfect, but it is good to know whatever the pitfalls are, and to think about whether they can work with that. Taking more than one test allows us to see what the similarities are between all of the test results, which may point to career possibilities that could be worth pursuing.
>
> Throughout the coaching process, our clients might have to go out and meet somebody, or they may have to go out and volunteer to see if they are going to like working in a particular sector. Especially when people are just starting into college, their minds are going at a million miles per minute. They are just learning about all of the opportunities out there. So what they want to do is see what it is going to be like after they are done with college. I advise people to get started on LinkedIn as early as grade 12. Get on there and create your profile, even with just your "starter" jobs, then contact people! It looks really impressive when a young per-

son wants to contact somebody in a more-professional field.

For example, if you are interested in going into accounting, contact some people who are in accounting in college, and even that are already mid-level in their accounting careers. Ask them if you can have a phone conversation with them—it's as simple as that. It is just typing an email and thanking them for taking the time to read it. You can tell them, 'This is who I am. This is what I am looking for, and I was wondering if I could have 15 minutes of your time to find out your career story, and what's it like to be in your job on a daily basis.'

This process will give you more of an idea if that is a job you would want to do or one you could not see yourself doing. This may feel uncomfortable at first, but it helps to remember it is your future you are investing in. Get started early. That is one thing I encourage young people to do—get started early. Get on LinkedIn. Don't wait until you're done with college. Get networking early.

You can learn more about Jennifer Bouley and the coaching her firm provides to college students at Bouley-Mak.com. The entire Money Champ interview with Ms. Bouley is available in the Bonus Material provided at the end of this book.

Career/Job Fairs and Job Shadowing

Once you begin to realize your interests and passions and

have begun to discover your purpose, I highly recommend attending a career or job fair or doing some job shadowing. College is much too expensive to go there and spend years "finding yourself" while racking up debt. You need to discover your "why," and then pursue the knowledge and wisdom to determine how you can spend the rest of your life living out your purpose *and* getting a paycheck. Attend career and job fairs to obtain the basic knowledge, and also in hopes of landing a job-shadowing "internship" or "apprenticeship." By doing this, you will gain invaluable knowledge, wisdom, and experience and, most of all, you will be able to determine if the job or position is really for you. If not, don't sweat it. Go back to the drawing board and take more time to really think about what your objectives are. Remember that this is your future, and there is no rush in completing the analysis. You want to make sure you take the time to get it right!

Gap Year

For many people who are unsure of their direction immediately after high school, a strategy that has proven advantageous for some is to allow a gap semester or gap year before beginning college in earnest. During this time, future college students can work hard to determine where their interests and strengths lie. They can earn money, travel, volunteer, explore options, and have experiences for personal growth. Students who already have been accepted into a college may ask for a deferred start date, keeping their enrollment secure while allowing for the delay. Some colleges even offer gap or bridge-year programs to help structure this time for prospective students and to help them clarify goals.

According to David Hawkins, director of public policy and research at the National Association for College Admission Counseling, taking this "gap year" may actually help students succeed in college since participants may be more focused, mature, and motivated for their undergraduate experience.[2]

UnCollege

A good resource to be able to find yourself and figure it out before you go to school—to go to school with intent—is a program called *UnCollege*. Gabe Stern, the co-founder of UnCollege, describes it as a resource for people who are interested in learning more about different alternative education options. UnCollege offers a gap-year program that helps young people build a roadmap for their higher education and beyond.

The UnCollege program flies under the banner of self-directed education. It starts with the particular area or areas a person is interested in or drawn to, then helps them explore and find direction. It teaches them how to develop and build skills, how to take on projects, and how to find audiences for their work. In essence, the students learn to take charge of their own education and direct themselves.

The program consists of three phases. In the beginning, the voyage phase, participants travel to another country to do service learning. There, they volunteer in some way— possibly teaching English or working at an orphanage or building houses. This involves them outside of their comfort zones and exposes them to new cultures. Doing this changes the patterns and routines that they have developed and places them in a new space, so that they can grow and learn more about themselves and the world.

After those first three months of traveling, discovering, and self-exploration, all of the participants gather in San Francisco where UnCollege is located. There, they live in dorms together for ten weeks, and take workshops on meta-level skills - things like networking, managing clients, negotiating, organization, and productivity. The students also work one-on-one with both a coach and a mentor to help them create a blueprint for their personal learning paths. Whatever it is that they are drawn to, they are given help to discern the important skills to develop to be successful in that field. They learn what important projects they can take on to showcase the skills that they have developed and how to generate an audience or a following for some of the work that they have created. They learn how to advocate for themselves and show off the hard work they have put in.

Finally, the program ends with a three-month internship, to mirror the real world as much as possible. They have to put themselves "out there," interview well, and work to develop the skills that are valuable for an internship.

Mr. Stern affirms, "The standard route is that you get out of high school, and you go straight to college. We want to make sure that people are going to college with *intention*. If they just take that next step blindly because it's what they are supposed to do, they might find themselves on the other end of a four-year education, in debt, without really knowing what to do, what they got out of it, or what they're going to do with their hard-earned degree. At UnCollege, we really focus on doing that active exploration before they go to school, learning about themselves and the professional world, so that when they get there, they know exactly how to use that resource."

The website is UnCollege.org. It also includes many free resources—guides for professional development and for self-directed learning. In episode 10 of my podcast, I discuss these principles in depth with Gabe Stern. That entire interview is available in the Bonus Material provided at the end of this book.

Purpose Leads to Productivity

In another recent podcast, I interviewed college graduate Sean Carney. In the following excerpt, Sean shares how he was able to find his purpose and finish school without any delays. Additional selections from this interview are found in later chapters, and the interview (in its entirety) is included in the Bonus Material at the end of this book.

TMC: At what point in your college career did you tap into your purpose and passion and figure out what you wanted to do after college?

Sean: When I came into college, I was dead-set on wanting to be a broadcast journalist. I was enrolled in Journalism for a year, but then I began to experience something that people told me might happen. They had said, "Sean, you might change. Don't be afraid to change your purpose and explore your passion because when you go to college, you find out a lot about yourself and everyone around you and your interests."

After the first year, I realized I did not really enjoy journalism that much and I did not really have a passion for it. I did some soul-searching and thought more about it, and I realized I had always been interested in marketing. So that's when I changed my direction. From that point on, my sophomore year, I've really enjoyed marketing, and I really enjoy radio as well. I've stuck with radio throughout all of my four years here. The experience I have gained from putting radio and marketing together has been absolutely phenomenal.

Honestly, college now is just too expensive to be switching majors four and five times. Maybe once, but *you definitely need to find your purpose and passion as quickly as possible, so you aren't forking out a lot of extra money*. Most people do not have the freedom to really take their time and figure things out because the more time they take, the more money they have to spend.

TMC: Regarding your purpose and passion, how did that fuel you to graduate in only four years? I don't know a lot of people that graduate in four years anymore. A lot of people hang out for five or six or seven…or even ten years.

Sean: It can be difficult to graduate on time. I see that happening with a lot of people here. It is difficult to graduate in four years, but worse—how easy it is to just stop going to college! It is really easy to just withdraw. So *in order to stay motivated, you have to have the right mindset about what a college education can do.*

A few years ago, someone told me, "Sean, just get a degree. It doesn't matter what it's in. Just get a degree from college. It shows that you can do higher education, you can do higher learning and you are experienced enough to get through a part of life that not many people finish. You can actually finish a college education." Those words really motivated me to not worry about figuring everything out in life, because every college student wants to just know everything about life as soon as they can. When you don't worry about that stuff, when you just think about getting an education and about furthering your own self, that will get you through within four years. That's really what has kept me going. Even if you graduate college at the end of four years and don't know if you are completely happy with the major you chose, it's okay. You did a college education and you have a college degree now. That one achievement puts you ahead of a huge crowd of people that never even got to that point.

Excellent thoughts! We can see how finding your passion in life and having a goal to work towards can help you to stay focused....and hopefully save you a large amount of money in the process.

Selecting a School

Clarifying *why* you are going to college and *the outcome that you hope for*, can definitely help to narrow the list of suitable schools to consider. Other important things to keep in mind when choosing a school are the total costs, any financial aid offered by the school, and the overall value that going to that school will provide (i.e., the likelihood of graduation, employability data, etc.). Many services offer college rankings comparing this type of information, including *Money Magazine* and *U.S. News and World Report*.

Often, students (and their parents) just assume that they need to begin college in a four-year degree program without thoroughly considering the implications or other possibilities. Many times, a four-year program will require students to accumulate much more debt than is truly necessary. Pursuing a two-year program first, and then moving on to a four-year school would likely save these smart students much stress…and money.

One of the biggest factors in the cost of college is the school (or schools) attended. In general, enormous cost savings can be had by choosing to go to a community or "junior" college for the first two years, followed by a transfer to a four-year college, as community college tuition and fees are *significantly* lower. Each state subsidizes its community colleges to keep the cost affordable for as many people as possible.

Wealth adviser Joseph Carbone of Focus Planning Group notes, "If you start with a good two-year program, and then transfer to the school of your choice, you could save tens of thousands of dollars."

Two-year community colleges generally offer the following advantages (compared to taking all of your classes at four-year universities):

- Lower tuition (in-state tuition, subsidized by state or other programs)
- Lower cost per credit for individual classes
- Open admission policy
- Convenience and flexibility in class scheduling
- Earned Associate's degree enables better employment if needing to work while later finishing at university
- Cost of student housing, meals, and transportation reduced by living at home
- Time for exploring options and choosing/changing majors at lowest cost
- Opportunity to increase GPA, if necessary
- Smaller class sizes for required general education classes
- Additional opportunities/sources for scholarships

For anyone concerned about a perceived loss of "prestige" by attending a community college for the first two years versus a private (or public) university for all four years, consider this: after that four years, your college degree will provide exactly the same amount of earning power, status, and "respect," except that you will not have burdened yourself with two additional years of heavy student debt - a wise choice, indeed!

When choosing a college path, an <u>essential</u> consideration must be the actual cost of attending a particular school.

Unless there is a vastly compelling reason for choosing a more expensive school (or the luxury of help paying for it), the best choice is obvious—the least-expensive college (or combination of colleges) that will get the job done.

Choosing a Major

Another Money Champ podcast features Nick Angelis, nurse anesthetist and author. In the following excerpt, Nick shares how he was able to find his purpose and make it through both undergraduate and graduate school without taking on a dime of student loan debt. Additional selections from this interview are found in later chapters, and the interview in its entirety is featured in the Bonus Material at the end of this book.

> In my very first semester, I stayed undecided/undeclared just to make sure what I wanted to do. I really wanted to be an entomologist or a bug scientist, and then I realized that, in general, very few companies want to hire them. I was also into theatre and things of that nature, but that is not really something that you can make a living from very easily.
>
> When I thought of nursing, I was thinking about the nurse stereotypes, and that really wasn't my style; but at the same time, I knew that I liked theatre and communication and science, and that nursing was sort of a blend of all of them. Then, in anesthesia, we do a lot of pharmacology and chemistry; there's a lot more to it than just nursing. Also, I saw that nursing was definitely growing as a profession, and I decided I want to be in a field that was starting a boom cycle.

So, I was undecided for the first semester, but eventually I decided to go for a bachelor's degree in nursing from Youngstown State University. I ultimately got my master's degree in anesthesia from the University of Akron to become a nurse anesthetist, which is what I am employed doing now.

I had gone to a private high school that was really challenging, so then by going on to a public college, the GPA really worked out in my favor. That is one thing that, many times, people don't think about—*when they go to a more expensive school, there is a lot more competition. You're not really going to stand out as much, especially in college where it really matters about the curve and who else is smart in your class.*

One of the books I have written is called *How to Succeed in Anesthesia School (and RN, PA, or Med School)*, and that is one of my basic premises—that we're so hung up on education in our culture and going to the "best school" and getting the most out of it that a lot of times, we're not looking at the real practical side of it. *We need to ask ourselves, "What is the value of the education I'm getting? Is it really worth the money I'm spending to get this degree?"*

As mentioned previously, this type of knowledge can go a long way toward helping a student determine his or her purpose and motivation for pursuing a college degree. There is a smart way to approach the financial decision that is such a big part of college - by *evaluating any intended major in light of its earning potential*. Pursuing a degree that has a more limited earnings outlook is perfectly fine and in many cases desirable, if it closely aligns with a student's passion and interests. However, the "prudent student" will also tell himself this: "If I know (or even suspect) up front that I am limiting my potential earnings by my career choice, I also need to limit my potential debt." To do otherwise is to invite financial disaster.

EDUsquared

In response to some of the difficulties prospective and current students face while determining which degree(s) to attain and which field to pursue—and as a result of his own college experiences—entrepreneur Daniel Haitz founded an organization, EDUsquared, dedicated to helping educate prospective students on *how* to go to college. It is an online video course that guides parents and students through that daunting process.

He notes, "When you are 18 years old in high school and thinking you might want to pursue physics or accounting or engineering as a career, nobody sits down with you and says, 'Here's what a physicist or an accountant or an engineer does. Here are the top three jobs they go into. Here is how much they earn. Here's what the unemployment rate is. Here's what a day in their life looks like.'"

In response to this fact, Haitz affirms, "I think you need to teach kids *how* to go to college or at least - at the very least - what each degree does and how much they could earn with each one. Up until now, there has not been a course specifically helping students evaluate college in terms of professional outcomes, effectively giving them the awareness of 'here's *how* I figured out *why* I should study the course I chose'."

To illustrate how critical it is to learn this information and to make an informed decision, he likens choosing a major and a college to buying a car. "When you head to a car dealership to buy a car, you know you are going to spend the money to purchase a car. But suppose the car dealer wants $20,000 from you before you even step onto the lot. You don't get to test drive the car. You don't get to know what color it is. You don't know how fast it goes. You don't know how much it will cost to maintain that car, or anything else that would help you choose. But the dealer still wants $20,000 from you."

In this comparison, a student is already committed to pursuing a college degree, yet is asked to devote huge sums of money and time to the cause, with limited real-world information to help them decide. A college education is one of the biggest purchases we make in our lives—the biggest investment we make in ourselves—yet we have been purchasing irresponsibly, without all of the facts.

EDUsquared is a fabulous resource for anyone looking at furthering their education. There certainly is a need for a central location that an eighteen-year-old (or anyone, for that matter) can visit to find out all the ins and outs of a particular job, helping them to decide if they want to pursue it. EDUsquared is the central location to find loads of information (on finding what the student's personal strengths are) and great strategies on how to minimize college costs.

The proprietary program of EDUsquared is divided into two parts - the *College Solutions Course* and the *College Savings Course*. College Solutions helps prospective students learn what is actually involved within particular careers and majors of interest, and it helps them to evaluate and match their individual strong points with the most-likely degrees or other educational choices (such as trade schools) for their strengths. It examines the general curriculum for the courses and classes the students might be required to take, the types of people that do well in that major, and the average salary and current unemployment rate for earners of that degree. The program assesses the top three jobs for that particular field of study, post-school options, and what a typical person with that degree does on a daily basis. Students are also educated in the basics of student loans, the differences between types of educational institutions, the labor market outlook, and how cost of living interplays with salary in different geographic areas and markets.

Once a future student has individualized his or her options and set a likely course, the second module of the EDUsquared program, College Savings, is focused on how to drive down the cost of the individual options that the student has an interest in.

As part of this process, EDUsquared demonstrates to their clients how to fill out the FAFSA (Free Application for Federal Student Aid) form. This is a form that current and prospective college students generally submit to the government for each school year to determine their eligibility for student financial aid, as well as their family's expected financial contribution for their education. The FAFSA is a complicated form. EDUsquared gives a full explanation and guidance about each line item on this complex form and recommendations on ways to maximize the amount of financial aid received.

According to Daniel Haitz, a critical part of cutting the cost of college is school-targeting - identifying and focusing on the right school. Simply put, the general rule is that those students most likely to receive a scholarship from a particular school are in the top 25 percent of students that apply to that school in a given year. This is determined by a student's average GPA in relation to the prior year's class (top 25th percentile), average ACT and/or SAT scores, and any extracurricular activities. Further, once financial aid from a school has been secured, extra negotiations can increase the amount of savings. Additional strategies to cut college costs are shared within the College Savings program, as well.

For more resources relating to determining your strengths and purpose for attending college, as well as excellent money-saving recommendations, the EDUsquared program is accessible at www.TheMoneyChamp.com/edusquared-course.

Future Earnings

A study of American graduates done by two researchers, Alan B. Krueger and Stacy Dale, replicated the findings of a similar study conducted earlier in Australia. Begun in 1999, the findings were released in 2011, and the study covered approximately 20,000 college graduates.[3] Krueger and Dale reached the conclusion that, from a future earnings perspective, *it did not matter* if college graduates had gone to Harvard or to Penn State, Princeton or Miami University at Ohio—the difference in earnings outcome was negligible. Effectively, a degree from the most prestigious university, compared to both "midlevel" and "high-level" universities only saw a three percent difference in earnings.

This begs the question, "If a student could get into Miami of Ohio or Penn State, which provide generous aid packages along with much lower tuition and a 'negligible' difference in ultimate earnings, why would anyone choose to take out $50,000 per year in loans to get through Harvard?"

In sum, determining your purpose and reason for attending college can help you choose the right college, potentially reducing the time actually spent in college and the money spent to do so, and ensuring that your degree will be as beneficial to you—and your future—as possible.

Much helpful information about discovering your passion and purpose, setting goals, and time management is available outside the scope of this book. I highly recommend availing yourself of resources to develop these important life areas.

Wisdom from...DEBT-FREE HERO Carrie Paetow

Growing up, I saw my family's struggles about money, and I knew that I didn't want that struggle. At the time, I didn't really understand that what people need to do is create a budge but, ultimately, that is what I ended up doing. I knew that I could not spend more money than I had in the bank, and I knew that when I received a bill, I needed to pay it. When I saw the number owed, I knew that if I didn't pay it, there would be interest and I would end up paying more...and I did not want to give anyone more than I needed to.

I knew that I needed to be focused on getting through school as soon as possible, but I went into my freshman year undecided and unsure, thinking I might like political science. A friend of mine hosted a radio show on the campus radio station. Another friend of mine and I listened to the show, and we realized we wanted to do that too. We went to the radio station the next day and applied for a show—we had a wonderful time doing our weekly show. Then I discovered that there was a campus TV show, and that also appealed to me. Truly, I had no idea why these things appealed to me because they really hadn't until I got to college.

I was involved in the campus TV show and, over time, I tried every single position: the teleprompter, writing, editing, and shooting. We hosted a mini-segment. Then I eventually worked my way up and became the host of the show. I worked on both the radio and television shows for five years.

During my years at college, I worked four or five jobs, studied, participated in track, field, and collegiate 4-H, and I hosted the campus TV and radio show. I essentially worked around the clock to save money, but it definitely paid off because I did not have to take out student loans.

I have grown up a lot recently. I think, before, I was just a clueless kid and had no idea what I was doing. I feel like people going to college now know a lot more than I did and understand things a lot more than I did. Regardless, there is a lot of trial and error, and I'm learning as I go. Honestly, I still don't really know what I want to be when I grow up! I'm still searching out and discovering some of my passions and interests.

I believe some things are very important for students during their time spent in college: finding a mentor, envisioning their future, doing their research and having fun!

Cultivating relationships is so important. Every single job or opportunity I have had is because I knew someone and fostered and nurtured that relationship. The saying, 'It's not what you know. It's who you know,' is so true. Surrounding yourself with motivated and goal-driven individuals—the people that are inventing new things and on the cutting edge, the people that are driven—those are the people to surround yourself with and partake in their energy; they will help you be successful.

Envision what type of lifestyle you want. I just did not think about this. For example, after ten years in television, I have realized I don't want to wake up anymore at 2:00 in the morning. My family and my lifestyle and my health are much more important than my job. Maybe that is not for everyone, but it's what I have discovered for myself. Those odd hours during the weekend are just not for me.

Research all kinds of careers, and figure out the basics. Aside from the money aspects, when does that job require a person to work, and what types of things will they be called upon to do?

I believe in job shadowing. Internships are very important, but job shadowing can have benefits for research—on a much shorter schedule. Asking someone whose job you are interested in if you can "shadow" them for the day can yield a great experience, and it only requires a day or two of that person's time versus a many weeks-long internship.

Another critical aspect of research is college costs and financial aid. For me, it worked best to attend a less-expensive school; I saved $9,000 per year over going to a state school, which was huge. However, that is not for everyone. If you have your heart set on a certain university, you will figure out a way.

> *Finally, have fun. You can invest in your future and be goal-driven, while still having fun and traveling and doing the things that you want to do. College is a great time to meet people and have fun, study abroad, and experience all the opportunities that you can.*

CHAPTER 3

SCHOLARSHIPS, GRANTS, AND OTHER SOURCES OF MONEY FOR COLLEGE

There are many ways to gather and put together the money needed to get through college. More often than not, it takes a combination of funding sources merged together to cover all of the necessary tuition, books, fees, room and board, and living and miscellaneous expenses. Following are details and hints to assist you in putting together a workable plan.

Student Financial Outlook

As you begin gathering information on colleges and financial options, it might help to organize the details in a chart like the one below.

Description	Cost	Grants	Scholarships	EFC*	Student Contribution
Estimated annual tuition and fees					

Description	Cost	Grants	Scholar-ships	EFC*	Student Contribution
Estimated room and board					
Estimated books and supplies					
Estimated other expenses (transportation, personal, etc.)					
Estimated Total Cost of Attendance Without Scholarship or Grant Aid					
Total					

* EFC = Expected Family Contribution EFC.

Family Contributions

For families who plan to assist their children with paying for college, an option is to accumulate funds in tax-advantaged accounts, to be used exclusively for "qualifying education expenses." The sooner you begin an account of this type, the more time it will have to grow. More information about these accounts can be found at IRS.gov.

Qualified Tuition Programs (QTP) – "529 plans"[1]

Individual states may establish and maintain programs that allow you to either *prepay* or *contribute to an account* for paying a student's qualified education expenses at a college or trade school. Eligible educational institutions may establish and maintain programs that allow you to prepay a student's qualified education expenses. If you prepay tuition, the student (the designated beneficiary) will be entitled to a waiver or a payment of qualified education expenses. Payments or contributions to a QTP cannot be deducted from your annual taxes. For information on a specific QTP, contact the state agency or educational institution that established and maintains it.

No tax is due on a distribution from a QTP, unless the amount distributed is greater than the beneficiary's adjusted qualified education expenses. Qualified expenses include: required tuition and fees, books, supplies and equipment including computer or peripheral equipment, computer software, and internet access and related services—if used primarily by the student enrolled at an eligible education institution. For someone who is at least a half-time student, room and board may also qualify.

Coverdell Education Savings Account (ESA)

A Coverdell ESA can be used to pay either qualified higher education expenses or qualified elementary and secondary education expenses. Income limits apply to contributors, and the total contributions for the beneficiary of this account cannot be more than $2,000 in any year, no matter how many accounts have been established. A beneficiary is someone who is under age 18 or is a special-needs recipient.

Contributions to a Coverdell ESA are not deductible, but amounts deposited in the account grow tax-free until distributed. The beneficiary will not owe tax on the distributions if they are less than a beneficiary's qualified education expenses at an eligible institution.

"GIFT" AID

Scholarships

There is a ripe field of scholarship money available in the world just waiting to be gathered and harvested. Grants and scholarships are often called "gift aid" because they are free money—financial aid that doesn't have to be repaid. Grants are often *need-based*, while scholarships are usually *merit or other qualification-based*.

Many of these dollars are awarded directly from individual schools to students, so a good first step is to investigate and apply for any scholarships offered by the particular college(s) you hope to attend. In addition to the money offered directly to students by colleges and vocational or trade schools, there is a vast pool of other college funding sources that also do not require repayment.

Powerful tools to use in locating these opportunities are the searches available at ScholarshipAmerica (www.scholarshipamerica.org), the College Board (www.bigfuture.collegeboard.org), CollegeNET (www.collegenet.org), FastWeb (www.fastweb.com), Cappex (cappex.com), and Scholarships.com (www.scholarships.com), to name only a few. Additionally, for those students intending to study abroad, many scholarships and grants for this purpose can be located through the International Education Financial Aid website (iefa.org).

Grants and scholarships can come from the federal government, your state government, your college or career school, or a private or nonprofit organization. Do your research, apply for any grants or scholarships you might be eligible for, and be sure to meet application deadlines!

Grants

The U.S. Department of Education offers a variety of federal grants to students attending four-year colleges or universities, community colleges, and career schools. Following is a summary of the basic types of grants offered by the federal government to eligible students.[2]

Federal Pell Grant

- Awarded to undergraduate students who have exceptional financial need and who have not earned a bachelor's or graduate degree. In some cases, students enrolled in a post-baccalaureate teacher certification program might receive a Federal Pell Grant
- Federal Pell Grant lifetime eligibility is limited to 12 semesters or the equivalent
- Award of up to $5,730 annually

Federal Supplemental Educational Opportunity Grant (FSEOG)

- Awarded to undergraduate students who have exceptional financial need and who have not earned a bachelor's or graduate degree
- Federal Pell Grant recipients receive priority
- Not all colleges participate in the FSEOG program
- Funds depend on availability at the college; apply by

your college's deadline
- Up to $4,000 award annually

Teacher Education Assistance for College and Higher Education (TEACH) Grant

- For undergraduate, post-baccalaureate, or graduate students who are or will be taking coursework necessary to become elementary or secondary teachers
- Must agree to serve, for a minimum of four years (within eight years of completing academic program), as a full-time teacher in a high-need field in a school or educational service agency that serves low-income students
- Must attend a participating college and meet certain academic achievement requirements
- Failure to complete the teaching service commitment will result in the grant being converted to a Direct Unsubsidized Loan that must be repaid
- Up to $4,000 award annually

Iraq and Afghanistan Service Grant

- For students whose parent or guardian was a member of the U.S. armed forces and died as a result of performing military service in Iraq or Afghanistan after the events of 9/11
- Must be ineligible for a Federal Pell Grant due only to having less financial need than is required to receive Pell funds
- Must have been less than 24 years old or enrolled at least part-time at an institution of higher education at

the time of the parent's or guardian's death

- Up to $5,311.71 annually (for grants first disbursed on or after Oct. 1, 2014, and before Oct. 1, 2015)

In addition to the federal money available, there are many other sources of grants for eligible students. States regularly have a pool of grant money to offer. Additionally, private industry, specific colleges, associations, and other groups often have grant money available to distribute. Qualifying requirements for various grants might include things like previous service in the U.S. military, being a specific gender or a part of any minority (such as religious or ethnic), being in possession of a special talent for sports or any of the arts, having a special circumstance or illness, or choosing to commit to a particular area of study. Thousands of these types of grants are available each year, just waiting for qualified students to apply.

Benefits for Military Service

There are five military academies, the Air Force Academy, the Naval Academy, the Coast Guard Academy, the Merchant Marine Academy, and West Point. Students who attend any of these schools and commit to at least five years of military service receive free tuition and room and board. Citizens who serve a tour of duty in any branch of the military are eligible for considerable help with tuition through the Montgomery GI Bill and other funds specific to each branch. The dependents of military veterans qualify for certain aid and assistance awards, through programs such as AMVETS, Survivors' and Dependents' Educational Assistance Program, and Military Commanders' Scholarship Fund, among others.

Membership in the various branches of ROTC – the Reserve Officers' Training Corps (ROTC) in college, or Junior ROTC (JROTC) in high school can provide substantial funds toward college as well. ROTC members take military science and training courses concurrently with high school or college coursework, and can apply for scholarships that cover up to the full amount of tuition and fees. In return, recipients must fulfill active-duty military service within their chosen branch for a specified number of years (varying between 3 and 12 years, based on the amount of the scholarship and the degree pursued).

College Prep Ready

Ashley Hill, a "scholarship search strategist" and the founder and CEO of *College Prep Ready*, offers some great advice to those on a hunt for college funding.

1. You have to be very specific. That is what a lot of people are missing. Make a list of what your strengths are, what your talents are, what your family background is, what types of things you like, if you have received any awards, and what your future career interests are. It's like a list of *you*, in really specific terms, on paper. Take that list to your chamber of commerce, charities, nonprofits, places of worship, and universities. They have a lot of what they call *external scholarships*, which means anyone is eligible as long as they meet the requirements. I also encourage students to check outside of

their own school district, and to look at other districts nearby.

2. Start local. The reason why is because the pool of applicants is automatically smaller, and your chances automatically go up, which is a good thing. "Local" is not just your neighborhood or direct area; local is also the city, the county, and the state. All of that is local to you.

3. Specifically for homeschoolers—most of the scholarships for homeschool students won't expressly be labeled "homeschool." But I encourage any middle school or high-school homeschooler to go to the high school or middle school in your area, go to that website or make a phone call. If a scholarship offered does not require you to actually attend that school, then it is open to you. Also, there are specific homeschooling scholarships. The biggest and best source for finding those is at the Home School Legal Defense Association (HSLDA). Among other things, they provide information about homeschool-specific scholarship opportunities.

4. The best age to start looking for scholarships, believe it or not, is kindergarten! The best way to find those funds, typically, is to look for scholarships for students under the age of 13. That will cover the entire group from 5 years up to 13 years old.

That 5 to 13-year-old age group may find it difficult to write an essay, so the search focus is on their interests. Start noticing what your child gravitates towards. If you know that they like to dance or sing, or maybe draw or something like that, then look for those types of scholarships. For example, Google has a $30,000 doodling scholarship, so if your child is really artistic, it's a long shot, but it could really pay off.

When your child is five or six or seven years old, obviously, they are not looking at college at that point but, in terms of scholarships, if you really start looking ahead—a couple of years ahead of their current age— you will have time to get your kids ready. For example, if a scholarship asks for twenty hours of volunteer service and your child only has five hours, you will have plenty of time to accomplish the other fifteen hours.

Overall, one of the biggest things in determining success in winning a particular scholarship is that scholarship judges are looking for leaders. They are looking for evidence of leadership abilities. For those (especially younger students) who have not had the opportunity yet to build up a portfolio that demonstrates this, you can lead *where you are*, like initiating a project or working with others on a team. A team is only as good as its members, and everyone has to be leading in some capacity.

In terms of whether application specifics or the essay is more important, in Ms. Hill's experience, the scholarship winner is generally the person who can closely align their application with the mission of the particular organization. The organizations are looking for people that "get it," those who have done their homework, so to speak. The best way to demonstrate that is to find the mission and keywords relating to that on the organization's website or printed materials. Stating your career goals in some way that can align with that organization's mission will likely increase your chances of winning.

These and other excellent strategies, for students in K-12, homeschool, current college, and all levels of graduate school, can be found at *www.themoneychamp.com/college-prepready*. The company also offers additional resources, and different levels of personal service, including "emergency" consulting and searching for those in a time crunch or up against a deadline.

State Scholarships

Many states, and even some smaller communities, offer scholarships to residents of their regions. These awards often feature minimal requirements, like being a "local" or maintaining a certain GPA or residency in the area for a certain length of time after college. For example, the Florida Bright Futures Scholarship program offers (to students who attain a certain SAT score) a "full ride" (tuition plus *all other costs* of attending college) or a full ride in conjunction with a particular school to almost any public or private college or technical school in the state.

Almost all states offer similar programs or other types of support. A good resource for learning about the assistance available to residents of a particular state is the National Association of Student Financial Aid Administrators (NASFAA) website, found at NASFAA.com.

College Track

College Track is a comprehensive after-school program that focuses on academics, student life, leadership, admission to college, and financial assistance for college (including "emergency assistance" if necessary). Mentors in the program work exclusively with students in "underserved" communities, starting the summer before their freshman year of high school and continuing through college graduation and beyond. Part of College Track's mission statement states, "We are dedicated to changing our nation's college completion story. We are devoted to building communities in which every student has the chance to earn a four-year college degree. We achieve our mission…through our singular goal: college completion for all of our students."

As of this writing, the program is available to students in many of the larger cities in California, Colorado, and Louisiana, with intention to expand to other cities over time. You can find additional information about this innovative program at CollegeTrack.com.

Universal Principles

Many of these scholarship principles apply internationally as well. I recently interviewed Jaideep Pathak, a businessman and MBA graduate originally from India, on my Money Champ podcast. He had chosen a Canadian MBA program that would take only one year instead of the customary two, saving time and money, but it was still very expensive. Owing to the many challenges of financing an education abroad, he had to borrow more than $75,000 at a high interest rate (including the posting of his parents' property in India as collateral) to fund his graduate education. To help minimize the cost, he had savings from prior jobs to cover his living expenses for one year in Canada (so he didn't need to borrow money for that purpose), and the school originally gave him scholarship money amounting to about 10 percent of the tuition fee, or $7,500.

Naturally, Jaideep was concerned about doing his best and getting out of debt as soon as possible. He said, "When I arrived at the school, I just started asking. A lot of times, students do not even ask…but I asked. I went through the admission process, and I said, 'Listen, this is what my situation is. Is there any way you could increase the amount of scholarship that you have already allotted to me?' Initially, the answer was no. But within three weeks' time, out of nowhere, I got a reply. I had been chosen for an additional $7,500 in aid (amounting to an additional 10 percent of the tuition bill). That was a big relief for me because I knew, based on my finances, that every penny counted."

Jaideep was able to reduce a part of his initial student loan debt through scholarships…and persistence. His story continues in Chapter 7, where we discuss in more detail ways to dig out of loan debt.

College Prep Genius

Faced with the prospect of putting two children through college on a very limited income, homeschooling mother and entrepreneur Jean Burk developed the extraordinary *College Prep Genius* curriculum, after first researching and successfully implementing the principles within her own family. College Prep Genius has helped thousands of high school students (including Jean's own children) prepare for the SAT, PSAT, and NMSQT, and actually obtain *full-ride scholarships* to their dream schools. She has been featured as a Fox news contributor, and serves as a frequent contributor to the Homeschool Channel, newspapers, magazines, educational resources and online publications.

One of the major principles of the course is that SAT, the PSAT, and even the ACT (which includes an essay) are all logic tests. The questions are purposely designed to confuse the students, and the wrong answers look very desirable. It is easy to fall for the trick answers. The College Prep Genius course teaches that these tests are nothing more than critical thinking tests, and how to read the questions correctly to find out what is being asked. There are other test-taking strategies offered as well, which can increase the likelihood of achieving a great score. Once a student has learned how to take a test, they can apply that knowledge to many programs. There is a crossover of information, and the principles taught in the course apply not only to the SAT and PSAT, but also the ACT, high school advanced placement (AP) tests, graduate school entrance exams, and even military and government hiring tests.

Ms. Burk has said, "Nobody should ever have to pay for college. And I'm not talking about the socialistic way that sometimes is promoted. What I am saying is that there are so many avenues out there, and people just need to know that they are there." Technically, you can go to school for free. It is just about getting out there, getting the knowledge, and not being lazy. Apply for every scholarship you can.

Approximately 85 percent of colleges will admit students and give scholarship money based on test scores alone. She has commented, "I don't know of any other way to earn the kind of money—hundreds of thousands of dollars in scholarships—that you can receive just based on a simple test score, just by learning how to take the test and doing well on it." Colleges increase their rankings nationally based on test scores, which effectively means that the higher the test scores of their students, the more money you get because you make them look good.

Ms. Burk has researched the many options available to students for getting through college, debt-free. There are a number of colleges that will give students free college for various reasons, provided they have the minimum SAT score to get into the school. In addition to the powerful program she created, she shares some advice on additional strategies.

- Some schools have big endowments—so much so that the schools are completely free for students. For example, the Curtis Institute of Music in Pennsylvania, Barclay College in Kansas, Macaulay Honors in New York, the Webb Institute in New York, and quite a few others.

- There are colleges that allow students to work in exchange for tuition. In other words, nobody pays anything and everybody works. The College of the Ozarks in Missouri, Berea College in Kentucky, and Deep Springs in California are just a few.

- There are at least 400 colleges that will give tuition based on needs. Now, the word "need" does not mean "needy." It doesn't mean you are poor. It means that is what they use, as a calculator, to decide, "This is how much money you need to go to this school." These colleges give anywhere from 80 to 100 percent of needs... colleges like Pepperdine or UCLA, Georgetown, and Northwestern.

If a student is looking for "outside" scholarships (not those which come directly from a specific school, based on test scores), he or she should make it a "part-time job"...starting to make scholarship searches, probably by ninth grade or even earlier, spending an hour or two per week and becoming familiar with what is available. As mentioned previously, there are actually scholarships available to kids as young as five years old! When we think of scholarship searching, we should not think just about high school. We should really get a jump on it because that money can definitely add up over the years.

When you are looking for just scholarships in general, start by looking around you, close to home. Start with the college that you are considering going to. Go to the local high school. They usually have loads of information in the guidance counselor's office that list various scholarships. Then explore news, sports, and volunteer organizations that are near you, like Kiwanis, the Rotary Club, the Lion's Club, and others like that.

Another of Ms. Burk's tips is to become very organized when embarking on a scholarship search. She recommends setting up a separate e-mail other than your personal one, to handle only the scholarship and college-related information that will begin coming in large quantities. Next, create an organizational system, such as a spreadsheet, that includes things like the scholarship names, their related websites and login information for those sites, each scholarship requirement (interview, essay, etc.), amount and terms of award, and the most important thing of all—*note or highlight each deadline*. It would be incredibly frustrating to work hard on a scholarship application, and then miss out on the money only because you missed the deadline!

She advises using the "secret words" when entering search terms into a search engine. Instead of just using the word "scholarship," for example, try inputting other words like "endowment," "foundation," "honorarium," "donors," trusts," or "fellowships." This type of search will bring up a multitude of scholarship money opportunities that would have never been accessed by only using the word "scholarship." She says, "We just tend to do what is normal, but when you do that, you fall into the same category as everybody else (and you are competing for the same money pool as everyone else)."

As suggested also by Ms. Hill above, before you really start searching, you can determine a "profile" about yourself, which can include things like your ethnicity, the cereal you eat in the morning, your parents' background, their employer, and what sports you like to play, among countless other factors and details about yourself. Start searching there: "Okay, let's see if there's anything having to do with someone who loves Dr. Pepper, plays competitive chess, or likes cereal…or whatever it is." One sometimes-overlooked avenue is that there are scholarships available to those who have disabilities (or whose parents have disabilities). You would be surprised what kind of opportunities are out there.

The main takeaway…**as long as students (or parents) <u>put in the time</u>, they have the ability to <u>get that money</u> and <u>get free college</u>.**

Jean Burk shares an inspiring story about a family who did just that:

People come up to me and say, "I am so glad I heard you speak three years ago because none of this stuff was on my radar. I had a sixth grader, a seventh grader, an eighth grader. But now we have a full ride anywhere we want to go." Then, on the other side, people come up and say, "I wish I had heard you three years ago because we are heading towards the end of high school, and we have not done anything and we are really, really stressed."

Here is a story that I love to tell about one such family. The father's name is Joe and his oldest son's name is Buddy. Back when he was in high school, Buddy went to a private school in Texas. He was an A/B student, a pretty good student, and he had taken the SAT two or three times, with terrible results. At that point, according to Joe, the guidance counselor had said, "You're not ready for college, Buddy. Don't even try taking the SAT again, because it's not going to increase anyway."

Luckily, Buddy's mom had heard me speak locally at one of the places where I was teaching a seminar. I mentioned that you can take the SAT as many times as you want; colleges don't care, because they just take your highest score.

So, she put Buddy in my class. He took the SAT again, raised his scores 600 points, and got $230,000 to attend Brown University for pre-med school. And he just recently graduated from medical school.

Now, that sounds like a great story, but that's not the end of the story. Joe's second son, Brenan, took my class and got full-ride offers to West Point, Cornell, and Purdue. Finally, his third son, Michael, just graduated high school and received the full-ride offer to Harvard. Hopefully, he is going to take that ride.

After all this, Joe said to me, "I owe you $2.2 million, because that is what all these scholarships are worth." And I said, "Well…just write me a check!"

Here is an entire family whose lives, whose complete destiny, were changed from having a kid who was told he would not make it to college to three kids who got full rides to Ivy League schools. Obviously, it was *well worth* the time and effort to this family for the kids to learn how to increase standardized test scores and do well in the scholarship hunt.

The College Prep Genius program is web-based, in an e-course format with a downloadable workbook. There are also live classes available, as some students are more productive in a classroom setting with teachers to assist. If requested, teachers from College Prep Genius will travel to a city and provide a two-day class, like a "boot camp." Students are given the e-course for review and encouraged to go home and practice to truly internalize the strategies.

This amazing system can be found at www.theMoneyChamp.com/collegeprep.

Additional Scholarship Strategies

Another excerpt from my discussion with Nick Angelis, detailing his approach to pursuing scholarships:

I was involved with a lot of different activities in school, especially because, at the time, I was coming from a more creative background. Even though I loved my major, I thought nursing was kind of dry and dull and boring in some respects. So, I did a lot of other activities in college.

I did have to study a lot, for sure. That's no question. But it was also very focused studying. I always had a goal in mind: "If I get this grade, I can apply for this scholarship, which means I won't have to work this job because the scholarship will pay for it. I can focus on my studies." So, it was more of a focus than just helter-skelter studying every spare minute and hoping it would all pan out in the end.

When you're in high school, you get advice on how you should tag your resume with lots of different activities. The thing that I have learned, though, is that you really shouldn't ever do something that you don't want to do just because it will look good somewhere. Life is too short to be in some honors' society, paying them $200 only so that you can write it down on your scholarship applications. I turned down a lot of different honor societies, including the prestigious Nursing Honors' Society, because I felt like, "I want to do something else with $100, and I really don't need more than one or two of these on my resume." I didn't think that either a college or an employer would necessarily select the person that had three honors' societies on a resume, versus the one that had "just" two.

I think it is an important point even when you're trying to think of things to do that look good on a scholarship application. Don't pick something just because of that. You need to find activities you like, and then people will see that you are well-rounded, that you didn't get good grades just because that's all you could do in life. You can manage to contribute to society, to the community beyond school.

As far as scholarships, I did not apply to every single one possible, but a lot of it was taking a well-written essay and revamping it for each individual application that I entered. I don't know if that worked well in grad school, but for undergrad, it helped me a lot to land the scholarships I needed. I explained how I live my life, and how that related to why I deserved that particular scholarship.

For instance, I didn't have jobs in high school, because I realized that would be a waste of time and effort. If, instead, I focused on getting really good grades, then I could qualify for the scholarships. Because I didn't work while in high school, I was able to be involved in various activities, which then looked better on applications, whether it was doing drama or sports or things of that nature.

Receiving free money for your education is nothing short of a blessing. The scholarships for students have grown more diverse with time, and there is such a wide range of scholarships and grants available now. Given the resources obtainable today, you can go to college, get a degree, and make a career without having to spend one penny from your own pocket. It requires only the *will* and the *effort* to do it.

CHAPTER 4

NON-TRADITIONAL CREDIT: SAVE THOUSANDS

In this age of the Internet, many innovative and effective approaches are available to earn course credits for college degrees. In particular, the requirements for general education courses can be met, in large part, through "non-traditional" credit routes. Many of the current paths are lower cost, and often with less time required, than taking a course through traditional means—sitting in a college classroom each day, studying a subject for an entire semester.

Most colleges will accept some form of proficiency examination credits, and the amount of credit allowed in exchange for passing these exams varies by college. If you already have a college in mind, it is a good idea to check the prior learning assessment (PLA) policy of that college before spending time or money working on studying for and taking the proficiency exams. If you have already accumulated some of these "alternative" credits, evaluating the transfer policy of any college you are considering attending can help you to choose the best school to ensure you receive as much credit as possible.

Advanced Placement and International Baccalaureate Courses

Although a few colleges currently do not accept this type of credit, many high school students have benefitted by taking Advanced Placement (AP) or International Baccalaureate (IB) courses. Taking courses of this nature, and passing the final completion exam for each course with a satisfactory score, usually allows students the opportunity to skip over but still obtain credit for general education college courses (varying from three to eight college credits, depending on the subject). The courses are generally free, but the exams require a fee (quite a bit less than what tuition for the equivalent college course would cost). In addition to receiving college credit, when making admission decisions, many colleges give additional "weight" to the scores earned in AP classes because they are usually more rigorous than regular classes.

Advanced Placement classes are maintained by the College Board, which also offers the CLEP exams for college students. Many students take advantage of this opportunity to earn early college credit; one-third of U.S. twelfth graders took at least one AP exam in 2013.

A **student with a qualifying score on an AP exam can save about $1,000 in tuition, books, and class fees and supplies, on average, at a public college and $3,000 at a private school.** Additionally, the "early" credits earned can help you to graduate timely.

The International Baccalaureate educational foundation supports the delivery of curriculums for gifted students, and is broken into four distinct age brackets. The diploma program is similar to high school, generally for students aged 16 through 19, helping them prepare for higher education. The program sets forth rigorous requirements for study in various subjects. Students in IB programs can opt to take subject exams, similar to AP exams, and the scores can then be submitted to colleges and universities for credit. Although not as commonly available in the United States, many high schools have started to offer IB courses as alternatives or replacements for regular honors or AP courses.

College Level Examination Program

The College Level Examination Program (CLEP) is a series of exams in more than thirty-five different subject areas that test mastery of college-level material. CLEP exams are taken by adults just entering or returning to school, military service members, traditional college students, or anyone who has acquired sufficient knowledge in a particular area and wants to receive college credit for it. Similar to the AP and IB tests, the CLEP exams are a low-priced and efficient alternative to taking an entire semester-length course.

ACE Alternative Credit

For adult learners and those students returning to school after being in the workplace, the American Council on Education's (ACE) College Credit Recommendation Service (CREDIT) connects workplace learning with colleges and universities by helping adults gain access to academic credit for formal courses and examinations taken outside of the traditional classroom. More information is available at AceNet.edu.

The American Council on Education began the Alternative Credit Project™ in 2014. ACE describes the project as "focusing on the more than 31 million adults in the United States who have completed some postsecondary coursework but lack a degree or credential. The project creates a pool of low-cost or no-cost, lower division courses and general education online courses across 20 to 30 different subject areas. Participating colleges and universities agree to accept transfer credit for these courses, allowing students to enroll with up to two years of credit toward a four-year degree."[1] This method could potentially save these returning students thousands of dollars. You can learn more about this program at AlternativeCreditProject.com.

Online Courses and Programs

In addition to their traditional programs, several well-known colleges and universities now offer individual independent study classes, as well as degrees that can be earned, *entirely online*. In many cases, the tuition for these classes and programs is equivalent to or *lower than* attending in person, plus the savings in transportation, room, and board for the degree program might really add up. There may be fees specifically associated with the online programs, so be sure to factor those in when comparing costs. These programs can offer great schedule flexibility and other options that may be unavailable to those attending the "brick-and-mortar" locations.

Innovative programs like the College Accelerator at Study.

com provide most of the required general education courses (and even a few, more specialized courses) for a reasonable cost per month or per course. These self-paced courses are generally transferrable for credit to a number of different public and private four-year colleges around the country. Students can complete these courses entirely on their own time schedules, from where they currently live—potentially saving thousands of dollars.

The Internet has made available the delivery of courses and information through such platforms as Kahn Academy, MIT OpenCourseWare (OCW), edX, uDemy, Saylor.org, and FutureLearn, among many others. Several of these courses are free of charge, and they can be used to prepare for taking credit-granting certification exams from CLEP, DANTES/DTTS (military), and other prior learning assessors.

Dual Enrollment

High schools in the majority of states now offer programs which allow motivated high school students to take college courses for credit (usually at a local community college) while still in high school. Credit for these classes ("dual credit") is granted at both the college and high-school level. In many cases, the college course tuition costs are waived for the high school students.

For example, at the College and Career High School (a public charter school) in Albuquerque, New Mexico, students work toward a high school diploma and a Central New Mexico Community College associate's degree at the same time, allowing them to enter a four-year university as a junior…or jump right into a career. Textbooks and classes for both the diploma and degree are free—a $6,000 savings—if a student completes an associate's degree.

According to one current student, "What CCHS has done is they let you experience what it is going to be like (in a career). Here, you get to explore a little bit. If you find something you like, like theater or mechanics or even nursing, it allows you to pursue it right away." She has taken advantage of opportunities to job-shadow and discovered a passion for the movie industry. The twelfth-grader plans to go on to the University of New Mexico and study film in the hope of becoming a director one day, and she is thrilled that College and Career High has given her a head start. "When you graduate, I think it is the coolest thing ever that you have a diploma in one hand and a degree in the other."[2]

CHAPTER 5

GENERATE ADDITIONAL INCOME WHILE IN COLLEGE

Countless students do not have other sources of financial help, and they must pay for everything themselves. Even for those students who *have* secured scholarships and grants, tuition, fees, and books are usually covered, but many times living expenses are not paid for. As a result, many students find it helpful (or necessary) to work at least part-time, or to find other sources of income while in college.

It is fairly easy (I would say, too easy) to borrow enough to cover both your tuition and your living expenses. The question is, should you? If you are able to manage working (even a little bit) while you are also going to college, you might make your life easier in the future by having to borrow less money now that will need to be paid off later. Some of your earnings can be used, as available, to pay for school as you go along, which will help with overall costs and, hopefully, minimize the amount borrowed. Other good reasons to work during college are to gain real-world professional experience, to establish yourself as a motivated person and develop good habits and, truly, to increase your motivation to stay in and finish school!

Throughout this chapter you will find some illustrations from graduates mentioned in earlier chapters, about how they found creative ways to provide for their income needs throughout college.

Carrie Paetow:

> "The school that I chose was very inexpensive, and I also just worked my tail off. My parents were able to save for that first year, so they paid for that and I did not work as a freshman.
>
> "The second year, I decided to apply to be a resident assistant, and I ended up getting the job. My room and board was paid for, plus I received the largest meal plan (an added bonus!). All I was paying was tuition in my second year.
>
> "The third and fourth years, I was being very frugal and working really hard. I had numerous jobs through work-study. I didn't really get any financial aid, except the work-study; it was great because you are guaranteed at least the federal minimum wage. That money went directly back to the school, so basically, they gave me the check and I signed it over and gave it back to them."

Federal Work-Study

Federal work-study is a great option for some students.

It is a financial aid option provided by the government through individual colleges. Work-study provides part-time jobs for undergraduate and graduate students with financial need, allowing them to earn money to help pay education expenses.

Here is a quick overview of the program provided by the U.S. Department of Education.[1]

- It provides part-time employment (only) while you are enrolled in school.
- It is available to undergraduate, graduate, and professional students with financial need.
- It is available to full-time or part-time students.
- It is administered by schools participating in the Federal Work-Study Program.

The Federal Work-Study Program emphasizes employment in civic education and work related to your course of study, whenever possible. If you work on campus, you will usually work for your school. If you work off campus, your employer will usually be a private nonprofit organization or a public agency, and the work performed must be in the public interest. Some schools might have agreements with private for-profit employers for work-study jobs. These jobs must be relevant to your course of study (to the maximum extent possible). If you attend a proprietary school (i.e., a for-profit institution), there may be further restrictions on the types of jobs you can be assigned.

If you are interested in getting a Federal Work-Study job while you're enrolled in college or a trade school, make sure you apply for aid early. Schools that participate in the

Federal Work-Study program award funds on a first-come, first-served basis.

You will earn at least the current federal minimum wage. However, you may earn more depending on the type of work you do and the skills required for the position.

Your total work-study award depends on:

- when you apply
- your level of financial need
- your school's funding level

How you are paid depends partly on whether you are an undergraduate or graduate student. If you are an undergraduate student, you are paid by the hour, and if you are a graduate or professional student, you are paid by the hour or by salary, depending on the work you do. Your school will pay you at least once a month and your school must pay you directly unless you request that the school use the money to pay for your education-related institutional charges such as tuition, fees, and room and board.

The number of hours you work and amount you earn cannot exceed your total Federal Work-Study award. When assigning work hours, your employer or your school's financial aid office will consider your class schedule and your academic progress.

The Federal Work-Study program is different, with different requirements, than just working for the college part-time job through the student employment office. Those jobs tend to be more flexible and are not part of a financial aid package. Either is a good option, depending upon individual needs.

Full-Time Benefits

For those students (or their parents) who choose to work full-time while attending college, becoming an employee of the college you are attending can have some great perks. Tuition and fee savings, in the form of discounts, waivers, or free credits abound at most public and private colleges. For example, Northwestern University offers employees up to $12,000 in discounts on tuition each year, and all of the schools within the University of California system offer some level of "tuition remission" or "tuition exchange" for full-time employees. Working full-time and going to school can be a big challenge, but the benefits may make the effort worth it.

Sean Carney:

> "Information about the Marketing and Communications School internship opportunities were presented to me before I arrived at school. They *guaranteed* internships and post-graduate employment, so that was a big factor in my decision about where to go to school.
>
> "I was lucky to find a better way to make a living—as a voiceover freelancer—rather than juggling a bunch of part-time jobs. I actually earn an income by doing what I truly enjoy, and I am also gaining valuable experience now for my career. This is a great little side part of my life that has been really successful,

and I am really happy about how it has gone because I know it's rare to have the freedom to create my own job.

"I found the freelance site "Fiverr, at Fiverr.com. It's a site where people who have certain skill sets can post an offer to do a job. Anything they have the skill set to do, they can post on there, and someone can order something that they would like. There are graphic designers, there are voiceover artists, which I am, web programmers—really anything. It's a great deal for buyers and, at the same, the sellers are getting compensated for something that they enjoy and that they have a passion for.

"It works like this: a small business owner who wants to make a radio commercial, which usually costs quite a bit of money to make, can go to Fiverr and type in "radio commercial" and get several results. They can pick whichever seller they like based on voice samples, and then they can place an order with that person, getting an extremely discounted rate, which is great for the buyer. At the same time, the seller is earning compensation from business that they would not have had otherwise.

"I have been doing voiceovers for about two years now and, within the past year, it has really taken off to something incredible that has allowed me to make that extra money to help pay for everything beyond tuition. Tuition may be paid for, but everything else outside of college—sometimes people forget to factor that in—must be paid for somehow. There are other payments that you have to make: a car or a cellphone bill, all the food that you eat…things like that.

"I have really enjoyed the flexible hours and the untraditional way I have made money throughout college. It's really fascinating. I am really thankful every day that I found a passion for that, and I have definitely thought about pursuing it as long as I can. I do plan to stay with it after graduation.

"As far as the time commitment, I would say that I always advertise myself, and I work as often as I can; it's really not bad because I can make my own hours. I spend about 10 to 15 hours per week on this voiceover side business on top of college and everything else, but I have learned how to balance it out really well.

"I set certain quotas for myself that I have to meet in order to get the bills covered, and I put a certain amount in the savings account every week. That generally dictates how much I need to work."

Talent Pool

Sean brings up some good points. There are many inventive ways as a college student in the current "information economy" to supplement your income—some that could follow you as side "gigs" into your career…or even someday become your career. Fiverr.com is a good place to look, and there are many other companies using the same overall business model that offer short-term or one-off jobs that are skill or talent-based and which usually offer flexible scheduling and a decent rate of pay. TaskRabbit.com,

Postmate.com, eLance.com, Care.com, oDesk.com, getBellhops.com, and Tutor.com are just a few.

Of course, there will always be more traditional part-time jobs, like working directly for the school, childcare or pet sitting, working for a retail business or an office, food service, summer sales, or lawn care, to name a few. Other avenues for income might include making and selling items on Etsy.com or at craft fairs, selling or reselling items on eBay, offering your social-media or graphics skills to local businesses, or offering your information technology and computer tech skills to individuals and small businesses. Turning your hobbies into money-making ventures can be a great way to bring together work and enjoyment.

There are plenty of ways to supplement your income while in college—it only requires some creative thinking, motivation, and determination…and good planning and time-management skills.

CHAPTER 6

MONEY MANAGEMENT AND SAVINGS STRATEGIES

College is a great time to explore, meet new people, and try new things. But, it can be tempting to live above your means and "try out" a lifestyle you really can't afford, especially when faced with an infusion of cash from a student loan. New friends might induce you to spend more than you might have planned, or you might have opportunities for travel or other enlightening (but expensive) experiences. The people you surround yourself with will likely have some influence on your spending decisions, so choose wisely!

You might have been able to borrow more than the cost of your direct college expenses (tuition and books and "living expenses"), and the remaining cash might seem like a windfall. *Please* don't give in to that temptation. You are on the hook to pay back every penny you have borrowed... plus interest. Your future self will thank you for being sensible and far-sighted enough to put off splurging until you start earning a genuine income, not increasing your burden of debt from the starting gate.

Savings Strategy

In another excerpt from one of my Money Champ podcasts, Nick Angelis shares some of his experience with first, saving money, and then, managing that money.

"I really tried to find a job that would complement my learning. Since a lot of it was a focus on getting good grades, and because I had scholarships, I did not need a whole lot of money. I thought if I could find jobs that reinforced what I was learning in the classroom, that should really help.

"Obviously, everyone is different. I worked with a nurse once who, on the weekends, worked at a really nice restaurant and pulled in as much money as she would have working as a nurse. That made more sense to her than to be an overworked orderly or something like it. However, I started out as a tutor for the basic chemistries and physiologies in pre-nursing classes, because all those classes build on each other. That way, I boosted my foundation as the classes got harder and harder. It was a good refresher course for me to brush up on whatever I needed to re-learn from that topic, as well as to earn some money to live off of or to save.

"Then, as I continued, I got a job as a nurse tech, so that I could understand the whole system. That was really important to me because at the time, I was very book smart, but I had no common sense whatsoever. We all have our skills and weaknesses, and I was dumb as a rock as far as clinical skills went. Honestly, probably after about six months with that job, I should have quit because I was pretty miserable, and I had likely learned all that I could have learned; there was only so much I was able to absorb. I probably should have gotten a higher paying job after that, but it was almost like an internship. Potential employers saw that I had this job for several years. I did well at it eventually, and I learned from it.

"Especially today, employers want to see real work experience. They want to know that you can mesh with their work culture. It's not necessarily that they fear millennials, but they do want proof that you have more skills than just whatever you got on a test. That is increasingly important, whether it be an internship or some way for you to demonstrate real skills that people will be willing to pay you for.

"Eventually, through working and saving carefully, I actually had some money to put away into investments. I guess that is almost unheard of for college students.

"It is difficult to choose the best vehicle because you need to be able to access your money. But at the same time, you also want your money to grow. The higher the yield you get on your investment, the more money you make it from it, but the more risk it is. So you really have to think about what happens. 'What kind of back-stop do I have if I lose these investments?'

"A lot of financial advisers, for instance, would make sure you don't have risky investments, for cases like those of students who cannot afford to lose. However, sometimes I do tend to veer toward riskier investments for myself, depending on the situation.

"Originally, for me, the best idea at first was 'laddered' CDs. Whenever it was time to pay for tuition, a CD would be ready for me to take the money out (principal and interest) and pay my bill.

"Then, as interest rates dropped, I ended up putting my savings into dividend stocks/bond type funds, which I still have to this day. That was a better way for me to save money, because I could draw on it whenever necessary. In fact, I did draw some of it for the 20 percent down payment on my house when I graduated from anesthesia school, and I was able to keep the rest of it invested and still earning money.

"So, it really depends. Right now, in mid-2016, I feel like high-yield bonds are the way to go. Many people are very scared, and they are doing terrible in the market. But if they would simply pick a company that is unlikely to go bankrupt, they should get a very good return without much risk. There are a lot of companies where they could get a 20 percent return within three years.

"Obviously, there are some risks to get that sort of return but, with the bonds, it's more straightforward. The bond investments will either go bankrupt, or they will pay you, as opposed to a stock, which typically, for students, does not tend to be that good of an investment.

"Also, there are other types of investments which can work well for college students or their families. Ventures like owning properties for other students to rent near the college can yield reasonable returns. There are many investors who take this route. For those who don't want to deal with the particulars and potential hassles of acting as a landlord to college students, oftentimes a reasonably priced property manager can solve the issue."

CHAPTER 6: MONEY MANAGEMENT AND SAVINGS STRATEGIES

Making the Best of It

Voiceover artist and graduate Sean Carney also has some great advice on saving money and making the best of the college years.

"I see many students work 10 or 20 hours a week or so in a traditional job; then they will spend that money on concerts or on going to bars or just hanging out. I know it's a part of being a college student that you have to enjoy—everyone needs to have some of that, but at the same time, it's important to set yourself up for the future.

"This is something I learned from my dad. He told me to look to the future, what's ahead, and always make sure I am saving for what's next, because you never know what can happen down the road. So, I make sure to have a savings account to back me up a little bit. Unfortunately, I don't know too many people that can say that coming out of college.

"To succeed in college (and life), you have to be open to change. You may go into college wanting to be one thing "when you grow up," and you might, at the end of your four years, finish in a career situation completely different than what you had planned. If you had told me when I was a senior in high school that I would be going into marketing or having a voiceover business, I would have called you crazy because it just wouldn'thave made sense to me at the time. I was that set on what I originally wanted to do. But, after a year in college, I changed. That was really significant to me. The best advice I would give to people is to be open to change.

"Also, it is advantageous if you are open to hearing and evaluating new ideas—open to different aspects of life. What you will likely find in college is that you meet a lot of people who see things differently than you do. Rather than immediately putting down ideas or things that people are telling you, it's really good to analyze those things for yourself and form your own opinions. College is such a great place to learn—not just in the classroom, but actually being in the college environment, surrounded by new experiences and people can really can help you develop and learn.

"Finally, what I feel most passionate about is to make sure you have a savings account. Make sure that you learn how to save and that you actually save some money! Take a course in economics. Take a course in the stock market. How does the stock market work? Think about and make a plan for how you can start saving.

"Many students aren't really thinking that far ahead, or think that investment in the stock market world is too much for college students and that no one has really tackled that. But it's your future that you are dealing with. If you can leave college with even a little bit of savings, you are ahead of most everyone else. That is money and experience that you can take with you into your post-college life and into a job. Financial experience is valuable anywhere."

Cost-Cutting Strategies

The U.S. Department of Education offers some cost-cutting strategies, a few of which we have already introduced, to help lower the expense of college.[1] For many of these suggestions, you'll want to follow up with the colleges or career schools you are interested in to get additional details.

- Set a *budget* and stick to it! Having a budget will help you compare anticipated college or career school expenses against your potential available income and financial aid. You also can use a budget to compare costs between different schools.

- College or career school costs can vary significantly and there are many schools with affordable tuition and generous financial assistance. Make sure to research all schools that may meet your academic and financial needs. To find colleges or career schools, use the Department of Education's college search tool, College Navigator.

- You may be able to get school credit based on your knowledge or life experiences, and you can manage your course work to reduce costs.

- Ask your school whether it's possible to "test out of" any classes. If you don't take a class, you may not have to pay for the credits.

- Some colleges give credit for life experiences, thereby reducing the number of credits needed for graduation.

- Most schools charge a set price for a specific number of credits taken in a semester. If academically possible, take the maximum number of credits allowed. This strategy reduces the amount of time needed to graduate.

- Some schools offer combined degree programs or three-year programs that allow you to take all of the courses needed for graduation in three years, instead of four, thereby eliminating one year's educational expenses.

Colleges and career schools may offer discounts on tuition if:

- you are a child of an alumnus or alumna (i.e., if your parent went to the school)
- more than one family member is enrolled at the school
- you are a student government leader or the editor of the college newspaper or yearbook
- you are an older student
- your family's main wage earner is unemployed
- you or a member of your family works at the school

Housing costs can add up. Here are some tips for reducing your housing costs:

- If you go to a college or career school near home, consider living with your parents or other family.
- If you live off-campus, consider sharing a house or apartment with multiple housemates to cut down the cost of rent, and carpool to save on gas and parking.
- Most colleges and universities sponsor resident advisor programs that offer reduced tuition or reduced room and board costs if you work in a residence hall.

You may be eligible for health care benefits through the

Affordable Care Act. Examples of these benefits include the following:

- Most young adults can stay on their parents' family plan until they turn 26, even if they are married or still living with their parents.

- If you have been uninsured because of a pre-existing condition, you may be eligible to join the Pre-Existing Condition Insurance Plan.

- If you are in a new insurance plan, insurance companies cannot charge you a deductible or copays for recommended or preventive services such as flu shots or other immunizations.

You can work part-time to pay part of your costs. Here are a couple of options:

The Federal Work-Study Program provides an opportunity to earn money while going to school. Ask schools if they participate in the program.

Cooperative education programs allow students to alternate between working full-time and studying full-time.

Most schools have placement offices that help students find employment and personnel offices that hire students to work on campus.

Taking small steps can add up. For example, you can substantially lower the cost of textbooks if you buy used books or rent textbooks (if you won't need the books once you finish the class).

Wisdom from....DEBT-FREE HERO Nick Angelis

When asked about his three biggest tips for college students right now, Nick Angelis had this to say:

One tip would be to find ways to make your major and what you're doing fun. This goes along with what I said about not padding your resume with boring things. For instance, I was in the honors' club. I really just did it to get the classes I needed, then I slowly realized I could actually get by with taking classes like geography of middle earth and exploring river landscape (it's just really white water rafting). So, college is really a good time to try new paths, figure out what's fun, and explore.

My second tip [somewhat] related to having fun is to not to make too much of a big deal out of things. You can stretch and challenge yourself to the point that you worry sick about every test, about everything that you're doing, and then you can't really learn. For example, the rabbit doesn't learn very much while it's running away from a bear. It's not thinking, "Is that a maple tree or is that more of an oak?" When you're too stressed out, you're basically trying to run away from the bear. If you trigger that fight-or-flight response too often during your college days, you're not really going to learn as much as you could.

Considering finances, what I said about focusing is important; you should have your financial plan set out beforehand so you know how much you can risk. You have to clarify your finances and realize what kind of back-stops you have, in case your plan doesn't work out the way you want it to.

A lot of getting through school successfully is perseverance and grit, but even perseverance can only go so far. You just have to keep your goals in mind. When you're down in the dumps and in a low place, you just have to see yourself getting out of it.

You do have to plan ahead too. When I was a nurse applying for graduate school, I was living for a while on about 10 percent of my income as a nurse, which was pretty pathetic. But I saw that by living that way, I could go through undergraduate and graduate school without any debt. I really lived like a pauper when it mattered. It was worth it!

Being able to focus and knowing when you can splurge on something is super-valuable—in my case, I still have those same habits from college, where I don't spend much money on anything. It really did teach me to budget…to save for the end, basically, as far as a life goal. I believe that if you sacrifice now, you'll enjoy life a lot more later.

CHAPTER 7

SOMETIMES DEBT HAPPENS: PATHWAYS TO DEBT FREEDOM

What if you have had to take out student loans? Are there special considerations or things to avoid? How can you get out from under that debt as quickly as possible?

The government will collect on your student loans for up to 25 years, and private lenders may be even more exacting. It is vital that you make your student loan payments a priority from the beginning. Maintain a singular focus and stick with it, regardless of your financial circumstances, until you have paid your education debt in full.

Student Loan Management Principles

- Although loan repayments are deferred until graduation, you can begin to make loan payments while still in school. It is definitely a good idea to begin whittling away at the debt as soon as possible. (If you make payments while your subsidized loan is on any type of hold option, the amount you pay will go towards the principal).

- If you do not feel comfortable making payments while in school, try to save as much as you can from each paycheck and put it in a savings/student loan repayment account.
- If you experience financial hardship, apply first for an income-based type of repayment plan, if possible, because you might qualify for a "zero payment" plan for one year and the forgiveness options available after a specified period of time.
- If you do not qualify for an income-based repayment plan and you need to place your loan on a hold, request a deferment first.
- Depending upon your particular loan, with a deferment, the government pays the interest on the loan, whereas with a forbearance, the borrower is responsible for paying the interest. If left unpaid, the interest will accrue and capitalize.
- Sometimes student loans can be broken down into different groups because of interest rate differences. If possible, make an additional payment and target it to the specific loan group with the higher interest rate.
- When on an income-based repayment plan, always select a deferment before a forbearance
- If your account is on a hold option, still try to send in some type of payment.
- Keep records of all payment receipts, special notes, etc.
- If you ever run into a situation where you have exhausted all of your forbearance and deferment time, use this as a last resort. Mail or fax a copy of your "necessity bills" to your service provider and special arrangements

might be possible.

- Ask if there are any new plans available.
- Always call in to inquire about your account no later than two weeks after requesting a change on your account

Repaying Your Loans

The following information is excerpted from the U.S. Department of Education's loan repayment guide, entitled "Repaying Your Loans,"[1] and it directly applies to the following federal student loan programs:

- William D. Ford Federal Direct Loan (Direct Loan) Program—loans were made by the U.S. Department of Education.
- Federal Perkins Loan Program—loans were made by the schools with federal funds.
- Federal Family Education Loan (FFEL) Program—loans were made by banks or other financial institutions. No new FFEL Program loans have been made since July 1, 2010, but you may have an FFEL if you were attending school before that date. Note: Although Perkins Loans are made by schools and FFEL program loans were made by financial institutions, these loans—like Direct Loans—are federal student loans.

For information about the repayment of private student loans (made by a bank or other financial institution under that organization's own lending program, not the FFEL Program), you would need to contact the organization that made the loan. For more information about repayment of

PLUS loans made to parents or loans made through a state loan program, you would need to contact your loan servicer.

For most loans, you have six or nine months after you graduate, leave school, or drop below half-time enrollment before you must begin making payments. You can use this time to get financially settled, to determine your expected income and expenses, and to select a repayment plan. Once you enter repayment, you must make your payments on time to avoid delinquency and default.

For each federal student loan you received, your school or loan servicer provided you with information about it, including the amount you borrowed and the interest rate. You also have the option to view your federal student loan information using "My Federal Student Aid" at StudentAid.gov.

As you review your borrowing history, you should make note of the following information for each loan that you received:

- The loan *type*. Since you may have different types of federal student loans, school loans, private education loans, or loans you received through a state loan program, make sure you know all the loans you've received. If you need help identifying your federal student loans, check StudentAid.gov/loans, or contact the school where you received the loan.

- The *amount* you originally borrowed and the current loan *balance*.

- *When* you need to begin repaying your loan. It's important to know when you are expected to make your first loan payment. For most student loans, there is a set period of time after you graduate, leave school, or drop below half-time enrollment before you must begin making payments. Depending on the type of loan you have, this period is called a "grace" or a "deferment" period, and it may last six months (for loans made under the Direct Loan Program or FFEL Program) or nine months (for loans made under the Federal Perkins Loan Program). Your loan servicer will let you know when your first payment is due.

- *Where* and *how* to make your loan payments. Make sure you know the name of the servicer for each of your loans and where to send your payments. The Department of Education uses several servicers to handle the billing and other services for all Direct Loans and for the FFEL Program loans it holds. Most schools that make Federal Perkins Loans also use loan servicers.

- The interest *rates*. To find the interest rate for your federal student loans, log in to "My Federal Student Aid," available at StudentAid.gov.

You are responsible for staying in touch with your loan servicer and making your payments, even if you do not receive a bill. If you don't, you may end up in default, which has serious consequences, covered in more detail below.

During your grace or deferment period, is the time to consider your income and expenses and create a budget. As you prepare to make your student loan payments, you will need to gain an idea of what your earnings and living expenses will be, based on your new job, and then create a budget to determine how much you can realistically afford to pay in student loan payments each month. When you have done this, you will need to select a repayment plan that best meets your financial needs and capabilities. If you haven't yet found a job, there are repayment options available to help you manage your student loans while you search for work. If you need help creating your budget, see StudentAid.gov/budget.

You have a choice of several repayment plans, including plans that base your payment amount on your income. The amount you pay and the length of time you have to repay your loans will vary depending on the repayment plan you choose. For more detailed repayment plan information and to calculate your estimated repayment amount under each of the different plans, use the Repayment Estimator at StudentAid.gov/repayment-estimator. Although you may select or be assigned a repayment plan when you first begin repaying your student loan, you can generally change repayment plans at any time by contacting your loan servicer.

The repayment plan options listed below do not include PLUS loans made to parents, Direct Consolidation Loans and FFEL Consolidation Loans, or Federal Perkins Loans. Information about repayment plan options for PLUS loans made to parents can be found in the brochure, "Direct Loan Basics for Parents" at StudentAid.gov/resources#loan-basics-parents. Information about repayment of consolidation loans can be found on the U.S. Department of Education Federal Student Aid website, at StudentAid.gov/consolidation. For information about repayment of Federal Perkins Loans, you will need to contact the school that made the loan to you.

Traditional Repayment Plans

PLAN	ELIGIBLE BORROWERS	ELIGIBLE LOANS	QUICK COMPARISON
Standard Repayment	All borrowers	• Direct Subsidized Loans • Direct Unsubsidized Loans • Subsidized Federal Stafford Loans • Unsubsidized Federal Stafford Loans • Direct PLUS Loans • FFEL PLUS Loans	• Time to repay: Up to 10 years • Payments are a fixed amount of at least $50 per month • Less interest paid for your loan over time than under the other plans
Graduated Repayment	All borrowers	• Direct Subsidized Loans • Direct Unsubsidized Loans • Subsidized Federal Stafford Loans • Unsubsidized Federal Stafford Loans • Direct PLUS Loans • FFEL PLUS Loans	• Time to repay: Up to 10 years • Payments start low and increase every two years; must be at least equal to monthly interest due; will not be more than three times greater than any other monthly payment • More interest paid for your loan over time than under Standard Repayment Plan

PLAN	ELIGIBLE BORROWERS	ELIGIBLE LOANS	QUICK COMPARISON
Extended Repayment	• Direct Loan borrowers with > $30,000 of Direct Loans, who obtained their Direct Loans on or after Oct. 7, 1998. • FFEL Program borrowers who have > $30,000 of FFEL Program loans, who obtained their FFEL Program loans on or after Oct. 7, 1998. • Additional eligibility requirements listed at StudentAid.gov/repay.	• Direct Subsidized Loans • Direct Unsubsidized Loans • Subsidized Federal Stafford Loans • Unsubsidized Federal Stafford Loans • Direct PLUS Loans • FFEL PLUS Loans	• • Time to repay: Up to 25 years • Payments (either fixed or graduated) in an amount to ensure loan will be paid in full in 25 years • Monthly payments lower than Standard Repayment Plan • More interest paid for your loan over time than under Standard Repayment Plan

The following income-driven repayment plans will set your monthly payment at an amount that is intended to be affordable based on your income and family size. Under all three income-driven repayment plans, your monthly payment amount is recalculated annually based on your income.

CHAPTER 7:
SOMETIMES DEBT HAPPENS: PATHWAYS TO DEBT FREEDOM

Income-Driven Repayment Plans

PLAN	ELIGIBLE BORROWERS	ELIGIBLE LOANS	QUICK COMPARISON
Pay-As-You Earn Repayment	• Direct Loan Program borrowers who: are new borrowers on or after Oct. 1, 2007, and have received disbursement of a Direct Loan on or after Oct. 1, 2011. • To be initially eligible, required payment amount under this plan must be less than what you would pay under the 10-year Standard Repayment Plan.	• Direct Subsidized Loans • Direct Unsubsidized Loans • Direct PLUS Loans made to students • Direct Consolidation Loans that did not repay PLUS loans made to parents	• Time to repay: Up to 20 years • If you have not repaid loan in full after having made the equivalent of 20 years of qualifying monthly payments, any outstanding balance on loan will be forgiven. Income tax may apply to any amount that is forgiven • Payments will generally be 10 percent of discretionary income, but never more than the 10-year Standard Repayment Plan amount • More interest paid for your loan over time than under the 10-year Standard Repayment Plan

PLAN	ELIGIBLE BORROWERS	ELIGIBLE LOANS	QUICK COMPARISON
Income Based Repayment (IBR)	• Direct Loan Program and FFEL Program borrowers whose required payment amount under this plan must be less than what would be paid under the 10-year Standard Repayment Plan	• Direct Subsidized Loans • Direct Unsubsidized Loans • Subsidized Stafford Federal Loans • Unsubsidized Stafford Federal Loans • Direct or FFEL PLUS Loans made to students • Direct or FFEL Consolidation Loans that did not repay PLUS loans made to parents	• Time to repay: Up to 20 years for new borrowers on or after July 1, 2014, and up to 25 years for all other borrowers • If you have not repaid your loan in full after making the equivalent of 20 or 25 years (as specified above) of qualifying monthly payments, any outstanding balance on your loan will be forgiven. You may have to pay income tax on any amount that is forgiven. • Payments will generally be 10 percent (for new borrowers on or after July 1, 2014), or 15 percent (for all other borrowers) of discretionary income, but never more than the 10-year Standard Repayment Plan amount • More interest will be paid for your loan over time than under the 10-year Standard Repayment Plan

CHAPTER 7: SOMETIMES DEBT HAPPENS: PATHWAYS TO DEBT FREEDOM

PLAN	ELIGIBLE BORROWERS	ELIGIBLE LOANS	QUICK COMPARISON
Income Contingent Repayment (ICR)	• Direct Loan Program borrowers	• Direct Subsidized Loans • Direct Unsubsidized Loans • Direct PLUS Loans made to students • Direct Consolidation Loans, including Direct Consolidation Loans made after July 1, 2006 that repaid PLUS loans made to parents	• Time to repay: Up to 25 years • Payments will be the lesser of: 20 percent of discretionary income, or amount you would pay on a 12-year Standard Repayment Plan multiplied by a percentage based on your income. • If you do not repay your loan after making the equivalent of 25 years of qualifying monthly payments, the unpaid portion will be forgiven. You may have to pay income tax on the amount that is forgiven. • More will be paid for loan over time than under the 10-year Standard Repayment Plan

Your loan servicer will provide you with a loan repayment schedule that states when your first payment is due, the number and frequency of payments, and the amount of each payment. Your loan servicer also will give you the opportunity to pay any interest that accumulated on your loans while you were enrolled in school and during grace or deferment periods. If you don't pay this interest, it will be capitalized (added to the balance of the loan).

You may prepay all or part of your federal student loan at any time without penalty. Any extra amount you pay in addition to your regular required monthly payment is applied to any outstanding interest before being applied to your outstanding principal balance. On your federal tax return, you may be eligible to deduct a portion of the interest paid. Members of the U.S. armed forces are eligible for special benefits on their federal student loans. To learn about these benefits, see "Military Student Loan Benefits" at StudentAid.gov/resources#military-loan-benefits.

Loan Consolidation

If you have multiple federal student loans, you can combine them into a single Direct Consolidation Loan. This may simplify repayment if you are currently making separate loan payments to different loan servicers, as you'll only have one monthly payment to make. Consolidation may also allow you to extend the period for repaying your loan, which may result in a lower monthly payment. There may be tradeoffs, however, so you'll want to learn about the advantages and possible disadvantages of consolidation before you decide to consolidate.

Deferment and Forbearance

Deferment and forbearance are methods for you to postpone or lower your loan payments temporarily while you are in specific situations that affect your ability to repay your loan.

Deferment

A deferment is a period during which repayment of the principal and interest of your loan is temporarily delayed. The interest is paid on the subsidized portion of a Federal Perkins, Direct Subsidized, and Subsidized Federal Stafford Loan. Deferments have very specific qualifications, requirements, and limitations. They can be granted for the following reasons: economic hardship, graduate fellowship, in-school enrollment, current military service, "parent plus," summer "bridge," and unemployment. More specific information on deferments, with a compete listing of requirements can be found at StudentAid.ed.gov.

Forbearance

A forbearance allows you stop making payments or reduce your monthly payment for up to 12 months. Interest will continue to accrue on your subsidized and unsubsidized loans (including all PLUS loans). Forbearance also is subject to specific qualifications, requirements, and limitations. The following types of forbearances can be granted: administrative, conversion (courtesy), economic hardship/excessive debt burden, medical or dental internship/residency, reduced payment (interest only/low pay), and temporary hardship. More specific information on forbearances, with a complete listing of requirements can be found at StudentAid.ed.gov.

Loan Forgiveness, Cancellation, and Discharge

You may qualify to have some or all of your loan amount forgiven if you work in certain public service jobs (for example, teaching in a low-income school or working for certain types of public service organizations). Additional requirements apply to receive these benefits. In certain other circumstances, such as if you were unable to complete your program of study because the school closed, your obligation to repay your federal student loan may be discharged.

The following information from the U.S. Department of Education summarizes the general circumstances where discharge of student loan debt is possible.[2]

Total and Permanent Disability (TPD) Discharge

A TPD discharge relieves you from having to repay a *William D. Ford Federal Direct Loan (Direct Loan) Program* loan, Federal Family Education Loan (FFEL) Program loan, and/or *Federal Perkins Loan* (Perkins Loan) Program loan or complete a TEACH *Grant service obligation* on the basis of your total and permanent disability. Before your federal student loans or TEACH Grant service obligation can be discharged, you must provide information to the U.S. Department of Education (ED) to show that you are totally and permanently disabled. ED will evaluate the information and determine if you qualify for a TPD discharge.

Death Discharge

If you, the borrower, die, then your federal student loans will be discharged. If you are a parent PLUS loan borrower, then the loan may be discharged if you die, or if the student on whose behalf you obtained the loan dies.

Discharge in Bankruptcy

This is not an automatic process—you must prove to the bankruptcy court that repaying your student loan would cause undue hardship.

If you file Chapter 7 or Chapter 13 bankruptcy, you may have your loan discharged in bankruptcy *only* if the bankruptcy court finds that repayment would impose undue hardship on you and your dependents. This must be decided in an adversary proceeding in bankruptcy court. Your creditors may be present to challenge the request. The court uses a three-part test to determine hardship, and *your loan will not be discharged if you are unable to satisfy any one of the three requirements.* If your loan is discharged, you will not have to repay any portion of your loan, and all collection activity will stop. You also will regain eligibility for federal *student aid* if you had previously lost it.

Teacher Loan Forgiveness

If you are a teacher and also a *new borrower* (i.e., you did not have an outstanding balance on a Direct Loan or FFEL Program loan on Oct. 1, 1998, or on the date you obtained a Direct Loan or FFEL Program loan after Oct. 1, 1998) and have been teaching full-time in a low-income elementary or secondary school or *educational service agency* for five consecutive years, you may be able to have as much as $17,500 of your subsidized or unsubsidized loans forgiven. Your PLUS loans cannot be included.

Public Service Loan Forgiveness

If you are employed in certain public service jobs and have made 120 payments on your Direct Loans (after Oct. 1, 2007), the remaining balance that you owe may be forgiven. Only payments made under certain repayment plans may be counted toward the required 120 payments. You must not be in default on the loans that are forgiven.

Perkins Loan Cancellation and Discharge

The following Federal Perkins Loan Program cancellations apply to individuals who perform certain types of public service or are employed in certain occupations. For each complete year of service, a percentage of the loan may be canceled. The total percentage of the loan that can be canceled depends on the type of service performed. Depending on the type of loan you have, and when that loan was taken out, you may be eligible to cancel part of or your entire loan if you have served as one of the following:

- Volunteer in the Peace Corps or ACTION program (including VISTA)
- Teacher
- Member of the U.S. armed forces (serving in area of hostilities)
- Nurse or medical technician
- Law enforcement or corrections officer
- Head Start worker
- Child or family services worker
- Professional provider of early intervention services

There is no standard application form for Perkins Loan cancellations. To initiate the process, you will need to contact the school that you were attending when you received the loan.

Late or Missed Payments

Don't miss a payment! If you don't pay the full amount due on time, or if you start missing payments—even one—your loan may be considered delinquent and late fees can be charged to you. If you are making late or partial payments, contact your loan servicer immediately for help. You may be able to change your repayment plan to one that allows for a longer repayment period or to one that is based on your income, or you may be eligible for loan consolidation, deferment, or forbearance. NEVER ignore delinquency or default notices from your loan servicer!

Default

"To default" means that you did not make your payments on your student loan as scheduled according to the terms of your promissory note, the binding legal document you signed at the time you took out your loan. To learn what steps you can take to keep your loan from going into default, and what your options are for getting out of default, you can visit StudentAid.gov/end-default.

The consequences of default can be severe[3]:

- The entire unpaid balance of your loan and any interest is immediately due and payable.
- You lose eligibility for deferment, forbearance, and re-

payment plans.
- You lose eligibility for additional federal student aid.
- Your loan account is assigned to a collection agency.
- The loan will be reported as delinquent to credit bureaus, damaging your credit rating, which affects your ability to buy a car or house or to get a credit card.
- Your federal and state taxes may be withheld through a tax offset, meaning that the Internal Revenue Service can take your federal and state tax refund to collect any of your defaulted student loan debt.
- Your student loan debt will increase because of late fees, additional interest, court costs, collection fees, attorney's fees, and any other costs associated with the collection process.
- Your employer (at the request of the federal government) can garnish your wages, meaning withhold money from your pay and send that money to the government.
- The loan holder can take legal action against you, and you may not be able to purchase or sell assets such as real estate.
- Federal employees face the possibility of having 15% of their disposable pay offset by their employer toward repayment of their loan.
- It will take years to reestablish your credit and recover from default.

Resolve Loan Problems Quickly

If you have a problem related to your federal student loan

(for example, if you believe that your account balance is incorrect), you may be able to resolve it by simply contacting your loan servicer and discussing the issue. Resources and suggestions for resolving problems can be found at "Resolving Disputes" at StudentAid.gov/repay.

Jaideep's Story (part 2):

On a more positive note, remember Jaideep Pathak from Chapter 3? His student loan debt experience is instructive. He was able to reduce his large loan ($75,000) by a small percentage with scholarship money, but he still had a long way to go.

He was paying a very high interest rate on his student loan from an Indian bank. Also, he had chosen *not* to work part-time during his graduate program, given that the MBA program was very intense, and he had chosen to focus exclusively on getting the best grades in order to get the best job after graduating.

He says, "I remember I could not go on student overseas study trips because I did not have the money, and I couldn't add more to my debt. I chose not to go, only to save money. It was as simple as that."

The big change happened once Jaideep graduated and secured a good job with a Canadian bank. He still had much of the massive student loan to pay back, along with a huge amount of interest accruing at a high rate. Soon after beginning to work at the bank, he took out a personal loan from the bank at a much lower interest rate. He then immediately paid off the high-interest loan from the Indian bank.

The last part of the puzzle was that he still had to pay back the bank in Canada. That's where the self-discipline and perseverance really kicked in.

Jaideep was determined to pay down the debt as rapidly as possible. Others questioned why he was paying it so quickly, because the interest was so low, but he was determined not to fall into the trap of the typical consumer lifestyle. He said, "I kept the student lifestyle. Even after getting a good job, I stayed in a basement apartment for six months. I could easily afford a nice apartment, but I was single and I realized I had a student loan to pay. So I literally saved every penny, and I paid it very, very quickly. I realized my priorities were different. I wanted to pay my student loans; therefore, I did not spend money where it was not needed."

Refinancing....or Not

Sometimes, new graduates make the automatic assumption that they should refinance their loans, but they fail to think about or investigate what they might be giving up by doing so. Private lenders do offer competitive rates when refinancing, but by leaving the federal system, you forfeit many of the associated benefits. When you refinance a federal student loan by taking out a loan with a private lender, you give up safeguards like deferment, forbearance, and income-driven repayment plans. Refinancing may secure you a lower interest rate, but you are making these options unavailable for situations in the future.

Debt Free After Three

In a discussion on one of my Money Champ podcasts, graduate and blogger Zina Kumok shared some insights about her journey to dig out of student loan debt. She graduated college with $28,000 in student loan debt, but was able to wipe out her entire debt in merely three years, on an annual salary of just $30,000. Her blog is called *Debt Free after Three*, and you can find it at DebtFreeAfterThree.com.

In an attempt to be more accountable, Ms. Kumok started the blog while still paying off her loans; she felt that writing publicly about her debt journey would help motivate her to stay under budget and pay off the loans as quickly as possible.

"I think getting out of debt is like dieting; we all know what to do, it is just implementing it," she says. "It is really the basics. I learned to live on less than what I was making and to put all of the difference toward my debt. Anytime that I had extra money, whether that was a birthday present, at Christmas, when I received a raise, or when my living expenses decreased if I moved to a new apartment or something like that, I just put that extra money towards my loans. Doing little things like that adds up faster than people might realize."

Zina commented, "I think sometimes when you are on a budget and you are trying to save money, it can feel so hard because suddenly you are hyper-aware of everything that costs money. It seems like nothing is free. Finding ways to enjoy life without being stressed about money is really important. I think it's always possible to find things to do that don't necessarily cost a lot."

It is true—paying off debt is like a diet. Everyone knows what they need to do, it's just a matter of doing it. Everywhere you go, in person and online, there is always a temptation to buy. Maintaining that willpower is probably the hardest part. Keeping the end goal always in mind can help. You know you can do hard things—after all, you made it through college! Apply that same focus and discipline that you used to get through school to get out of debt. Remember how good it felt to finish your classes and to graduate? Getting that debt paid off will feel just as good!

Debt Free after Three offers a self-paced course, a "holistic approach," showing step-by-step how Ms. Kumok paid off her loans, as well as teaching about the basics of personal finance and financial literacy. You can find a link to the complete Money Champ interview with Zina Kumok in the Bonus Material at the end of this book.

> *Wisdom from...DEBT-FREE HERO Jaideep Pathak*
>
> *Jaideep Pathak was asked what thoughts he would share with students who are getting ready to take out large student loans to pay for college. His advice is enlightening.*
>
> *First, they need to be very clear. People need to have a clear understanding of debt. It's very easy to get into any program, any fancy school, with a massive amount of student loan. But people need to have a clear picture. What will happen once the repayment schedule kicks in? Are they prepared for that?*
>
> *I've seen a lot of students who are completely unaware of these*

realities of life. But even more important than that, I think students need to have their priorities very straight. If they're going to school, they must strive for good grades, and if they are going to school, they must be critically aware of their own realities.

For example, I am a first-generation immigrant. I had no family backing at all, so I knew my reality. I knew that if something went wrong, I could not pick up the phone and call my family for more money. I could not do that. So I had to be very careful with my priorities. After having gone through that process, I completely eliminated all the debt. Today I have no debt whatsoever of any kind—even a mortgage. I came to Canada with a negative equity of around $60,000, but I have not only eliminated that, I have built significant equity by means of a house here.

So, the lesson is that one needs to understand the relationship with debt. I'm not saying debt is always bad, but you need to be very careful and ask yourself, "Can I put down money out of my own pockets? Why am I taking on this debt?"

There's no better feeling than not having debt—being debt-free. It's an amazing feeling to have, to not have any debt. Self-control and perseverance are the keys.

CHAPTER 8

FINAL THOUGHTS

- Now that you have finished reading this book, I hope you have gained a clear understanding that the "conventional" thinking about student loan debt has gotten us into a collective mess and negatively impacted the financial futures of millions of people.

- My wish is that you take the information and strategies in this book to heart, and that you are motivated to take the steps necessary to choose wisely and to enable the brightest financial future for yourself. I hope you will truly win in the financial ring!

- You <u>CAN</u> achieve the goal of "Getting a College Degree—Debt Free." I look forward to receiving your questions and comments at Nick@theMoneyChamp.com.

BONUS MATERIAL:

Money Champ podcast interview with Carrie Paetow:
http://themoneychamp.com/carrie-paetow

Money Champ podcast interview with Sean Carney:
http://themoneychamp.com/sean-carney

Money Champ podcast interview with Jaideep Pathak:
http://themoneychamp.com/Jaideep-Pathak

Money Champ podcast interview with Nick Angelis:
http://themoneychamp.com/nick-angelis

Money Champ podcast interview with Jennifer Bouley of Bouley-Mak Consulting:
http://themoneychamp.com/bouley-mak

Money Champ podcast interview with Daniel Haitz of EDUsquared:
http://themoneychamp.com/Daniel-Haitz

Money Champ podcast interview with Ashley Hill of College Prep Ready:
http://themoneychamp.com/college-prep-ready

Money Champ podcast interview with Jean Burk of College Prep Genius:
http://themoneychamp.com/college-prep-genius

Money Champ podcast interview with Gabe Stern of UnCollege:
http://themoneychamp.com/Gabe-Stern

Money Champ podcast interview with Zina Kumok of Debt Free after Three:
http://themoneychamp.com/Zina-Kumok

The Keys to Transformation and Peace

by Nick Blair, The Money Champ©

I am very passionate about sharing how I discovered my "Why" in life, and how I use my purpose to fuel my passion to empower others to succeed. Many of us lead stressful and complicated lives. Never before have we been so stressed out, burned out, and worked so hard—only to feel it taking a toll on our health, relationships, and the quality of our lives. There is no better time than now to improve and transform your life forever!

Whether you realize it or not, most everything you do on a daily basis, from your recurring thoughts to your patterns of living and the way you take care of yourself, is essentially just the way you have always done it in the past.

This is not the part where I tell you there is a magic wand and all you have to do is close your eyes and blink to make it all magically align. But if you are sick and tired of doing the same thing and not getting a different outcome—of living below your potential—you will need a paradigm shift. A paradigm shift is a fundamental change in approach or underlying assumptions, or a time when the usual and accepted way of doing or thinking about something changes completely. It is only when you closely inspect and examine yourself through self-management, and undergo a paradigm shift and apply these techniques to your daily life, that you will begin to shift into an unbelievable sense of fulfillment. You will operate in a new, rewarding lifestyle because you will be operating within your purpose.

I have achieved peace and a sense of fulfillment in my life

by possessing these four components: Spirituality, Purpose, Wisdom and Perseverance. I have realized that I can only do so much on my own. I needed *spirituality* in my life because I knew I would be tested and would need to tap into that realm for guidance, assistance, and strength. You must know your *purpose* in life, or you will live your life feeling unfulfilled, constantly looking for something or someone to fill that void. Knowing your purpose is the key to maximizing your potential and "dying empty"! I understood that I needed *wisdom* in order to make the right decisions at the right time. Lastly, I gained *perseverance*, because sometimes it takes fighting for what you want (not just figuratively). John Burroughs said it best, "For anything worth having, one must pay the price; and the price is always work, patience, love, and self-sacrifice." You must have perseverance in order to pay the price, complete the work, exercise patience when needed, love those who hate you, and sacrifice whatever it takes to achieve your desired outcomes.

Principles to Live By

#1: Self-Worth

How you think about yourself and what you say dictates your life.

Do you ever feel like there is a calling in your soul that needs to be heard? If you were to really look at how you connect on a daily basis with your higher consciousness and/or self and the universe as a whole... what percentage of your days are spent tuning in and reconnecting to your spirit and exploring all that is available to you?

If you are struggling to find balance in your life, the answer to that question is probably "not too often." It is a tragedy that, as a society, we are in danger of becoming spiritually bankrupt. A lot of our daily focus tends to be upon things and situations outside of ourselves, not really being in tune with all the wondrous nuances and opportunities that exist in almost every person, place, and thing we encounter and experience.

One of the most important principles in creating a life with balance is creating your own unique spiritual connection that reflects your core beliefs and desired lifestyle. There are truly endless ways to find and create spirituality in your everyday life. There are daily ways to practice having a deeper connection to all that is.

There are so many ways to learn how to tune in and start creating more consciousness in your day-to-day life. The most important part is just beginning... to practice and learn how to be present and live in the moment!

When you live in the past, you cannot live in the now or create your future. The more you learn to tune in and create more and more conscious awareness, the more you will be able to tune in and deepen your spiritual connection for yourself and your life.

#2: Knowledge

You have probably heard the saying that people perish for the lack of knowledge. I believe this to be very true. For example, if you want to be a millionaire, you must have some knowledge of how to go about making a million dollars. You can have all the desire in the world to be a millionaire, but without the knowledge, it is going to be hard (if not impossible) to acquire that million dollars, unless you inherit it or win the lottery. Then, you still need to have some knowledge of how to make that money work for you, at least to maintain it if not to multiply it into more. How many times do you hear of someone winning the lottery, then losing all of that money within a few months' or years' time? I feel so sad for those people!

You see, the same thing applies to losing weight, or being wealthy, or being successful, or having what you want. You must have the knowledge about what to do, not only to make it happen, but to continue to make it happen. What kind of exercising is best for accomplishing your goal? What do you need to be eating on a regular basis? What steps must be completed to reach your goal? You have got to do what it takes to acquire the proper knowledge to be successful. You can have some knowledge on how to make a million dollars, but if it is the wrong knowledge or information, you are just wasting your time. You have to have the peace of mind to know that you have the right knowledge and information.

#3: Desire

You must have a desire for what it is you want to do. YOU must want it, not someone else. You must have a desire for what you want to accomplish. For you to have invested money to purchase this book and to have read this much shows that you have the desire to be wise in getting through college. You must have the desire for change, and you must have the desire to be successful. Desire usually comes hand-in-hand with purpose and passion. You will have a desire for something when you discover your purpose and have a passion for it. Wherever that purpose and passion is, there will also come excitement. When you desire something so much, you will usually develop a passion for that and be excited about going to attain it. You see, that desire is a must, but it is not enough. It takes more than that. You must tap into that spiritual place or realm for guidance and assistance. Think about it.

#4: Giving Back

Philanthropy is the act of "giving back" out of your time, services, goods, or money for a specific, noteworthy cause or just because you are grateful for your own blessings. There are so many important levels of what this means to the bigger picture. At the end of the day, what matters is what this means *to you* and how your ability to give back can make a significant impact.

I often think about where we are in the world today and the health of our nation as a whole. In this challenging time we are in, we seem to be truly out of balance as we try to move forward in a productive effort to thrive. Everyone is talking about "crisis" instead of opportunity, and the media encourages us to think about the negative emotional drivers, without much emphasis on those who are making a positive impact. The real question should be, "What can I do to have a positive effect on the world around me?"

Commitments

Commitments are an ongoing quality of life. They speak to the essence of the life that we are creating. There are no specifics; no measurable time or quantity limits as there are with goals. Therefore, there are no limits placed upon your achievements. Commitments have to do with the state or the kind of being you want to create in your life.

"I am committed to enjoying and being creative in my work," and "I am committed to being kind to myself by watching how and what I eat," are examples of commitments in the areas of Profession and Physical Well-Being respectively.

Think about and *write down what you are committed to* creating in the following areas of your life:

- Living your purpose and operating in your passion

- Utilizing your talents and gifts while including your core values and characteristic traits

When you have done this, you can formulate specific goals to help you fulfill your commitments.

Goals

Write in the form of a statement.

Are my goals in alignment with my values and commitments?

1. _____

2. _____

3. _____

4. _____

5. _____

6. _____

7. _____

8. _____

9. _____

10. _____

Putting Goals into ACTION

Name of Goal:

_____

Vision Statement:

_____

_____

Start Date: _____ (Begin working toward goal)

Target Date: _____ (Desired date of accomplishment)

Completion Date: _____ (Actual date of accomplishment)

Monthly Action Plan (M.A.P)

How will I go about reaching my goals? What method(s) will I use?

The steps I will take:

1. _____

2. _____

3. _____

4. _____

5. _____

6. _____

7. _____

8. _____

9. _____

10. _____

Expected Results

How will I feel when I achieve my goal?

1. _____

2. _____

3. _____

4. _____

5. _____

6. _____

7. _____

8. _____

9. _____

10. _____

Benefits from Achieving Goal

How will this get me closer to my final desired outcome? What positive results will I enjoy?

1. _____

2. _____

3. _____

4. _____

5. _____

6. _____

7. _____

8. _____

9. _____

10. _____

Tracking: How am I going to measure my results?

Potential Obstacles: What obstacles do I anticipate having or am I going through currently?

Solutions and Opportunities: What will I do to make my dreams a reality?

Goal Completion

Number	Target Date	Date of Completion
1		
2		
3		
4		
5		

Number	Target Date	Date of Completion
6		
7		
8		
9		
10		

REFERENCES

Chapter 1

1. Bureau of Labor Statistics, U.S. Department of Labor, *The Economics Daily*, "College tuition and fees increase 63 percent since January 2006," http://www.bls.gov/opub/ted/2016/college-tuition-and-fees-increase-63-percent-since-january-2006.htm.

2. http://www.collegedata.com/cs/content/content_payarticle_tmpl.jhtml?articleId=10064

3. https://studentaid.ed.gov/sa/about/data-center/student/portfolio

4. https://www.newyorkfed.org/studentloandebt/index.html

5. American Student Assistance, *Life Delayed: The Impact of Student Debt on the Daily Lives of Young Americans*, 2013. http://www.asa.org/site/assets/files/3793/life_delayed.pdf

6. National Foundation for Credit Counseling, *The 2016 Consumer Financial Literacy Survey*, Washington, D.C., 2016. https://nfcc.org/wp-content/uploads/2016/04/NFCC_BECU_2016-FLS_datasheet-with-key-findings_041516.pdf

Chapter 2

1. *www.collegeatlas.org/college-dropout.html*

2. http://www.princetonreview.com/study-abroad/col-

lege-abroad/gap-year

3. Krueger, A.B. and Dale, S. "Estimating the Return to College Selectivity of the Career Using Administrative Earning Data," *Journal of Human Resources*, Spring 2014, vol. 49, no. 2, pp. 323-358.

Chapter 3

1. IRS.gov, *Tax Benefits for Education: Information Center*, "Savings Plans," https://www.irs.gov/uac/tax-benefits-for-education-information-center

2. U.S. Department of Education, Federal Student Aid, Customer Experience Office, *Types of Aid: Federal Student Grant Programs*, Washington, D.C., 2015. https://studentaid.ed.gov/sa/sites/default/files/federal-grant-programs.pdf

Chapter 4

1. http://www.alternativecreditproject.com

2. https://www.abqjournal.com/839432/cchs-gives-kids-a-career-jump-start.html

Chapter 5

1. https://studentaid.ed.gov/sa/types/work-study

Chapter 6

1. U.S. Department of Education, Federal Student Aid, Customer Experience Office, *Prepare for College: Understanding College Costs*, Washington, D.C., 2015. https://studentaid.ed.gov/sa/prepare-for-college/choos-

ing-schools/consider/costs

Chapter 7

1. U.S. Department of Education, Federal Student Aid, Customer Experience Office, *Repaying Your Loans*, Washington, D.C., 2015. https://studentaid.ed.gov/sa/sites/default/ files/repaying-your-loans.pdf

2. U.S. Department of Education, Federal Student Aid, Customer Experience Office, *Forgiveness, Cancellation, and Discharge*, Washington, D.C., 2015. https://studentaid.ed.gov/sa/repay-loans/forgiveness-cancellation

3. U.S. Department of Education, Federal Student Aid, Customer Experience Office, *Understanding Default*, Washington, D.C., 2015. https://studentaid.ed.gov/ sa/repay-loans/default#consequences

Appendix